DON DUNFORD:

JUST A COUNTRY BOY

Edited By
Linda Hudson Hoagland

ISBN: 978-0-692-35093-5
Copyright © 2014 Don Dunford: Just A Country Boy
Printed in the United States of America
Printing by Clinch Valley Printing
                    North Tazewell, Virginia

Table of Contents

Delegate Don Dunford

"Some people say politics is dirty, Don says only some people in politics are dirty."

"Too many elected officials spend time trying to be re-elected rather than doing the job they were elected to do."

To my dear wife Nancy and darling daughter Donna –

And – to friends – many, many, more than recognized here –

Don Dunford

MEMORIES UPDATED

For several years, Don Dunford has been trying to convince Jim Ramey of Ramey Auto Group, to tell his story but it was to no avail. Because Jim Ramey refuses to tell his story, Don felt an obligation to offer to all of Jim's family and friends one of the more interesting parts of Jim Ramey's eventful life.

During a tour of duty in Korea, Jim Ramey was the driver of the doughnut truck for the Red Cross. It was his duty to deliver the sweet treats to the soldiers on his specified route no matter what the possible dangers might be ahead of him and his load of doughnuts.

Jim Ramey was proud of what he contributed to make the American soldiers a little less homesick who were stationed in Korea during the conflict, called the Korean War by most of those who played a part. Jim said that he enjoyed every bit of what he did for the soldiers even though there were a couple of times when he was scared that he might not survive the delivery route.

Jim Ramey during tour of Korean War.

In Jim's words, "You know, there I was, and the girls I was driving were old timers, maybe 26 or 27. I was happy to be around Americans all of the time."

When Jim returned from Korea he went back to high school where he and Don were teammates on the 1951 defeated football team at Tazewell High School.

He was so proud in fact, that years later during a Chevrolet meeting in Japan, he made it his mission to board an airplane to head for Korea.

Jim Ramey & Don Dunford

It was his goal to return to his doughnut truck route and travel the road once again.

He climbed into a limousine instructing the driver each step of the way following the path his doughnut truck had taken many years earlier.

That was the itch that Jim Ramey was finally able to scratch. It was also an item removed from his bucket list.

Jim Ramey has accomplished many goals in life and that all began with the help of his mother who saved every penny of $40.00 he mailed to her every payday.

With the meager savings of $1,500.00 that had been accumulated by the time he was discharged from the army, Jim Ramey started on his road to automotive dealerships by purchasing three used cars for resale.

One night Don and Jim were riding around Tazewell surveying the area for needs. Jim pulled into the Walker Chevrolet Dealership and

Pam, Donna, Jim, Jimmy and Jennifer

said, "Don, I am going to buy Walker out. However, I need $10,000 more in order to satisfy the bank and make the deal work. Since you just sold a piece of property, would you loan me $10.000? You did and I did – no note, not even a handshake. You just handed me the check."

Sometime after Jim Ramey bought the Walker Dealership, he was invited to Princeton for a dinner being addressed by a motivational speaker. Jim took Don with him and to this day they remember highlights of the speech given by a man who had a speech impediment. For one hour, the speaker mesmerized the audience and at the end of his talk he told the crowd:

"Show me a man who can make a decision and I will show you a man who can make a million dollars."

Jim & Katye

Of course, Jim Ramey is a car salesman and has been for many years. One of his memorable quotes is, "You can always sleep in your car but you can't drive your house."

Don recalls a beautiful moment at the wedding of Jim Ramey's son, Jimmy and Jessica, the daughter of Rick Chitwood, when Don's daughter, Donna Dunford Biggs, entranced the wedding guests with music from her harp.

Another man who deserves recognition as a contributor to the success of many aspects of Tazewell County is Rick Chitwood, and Don is proud to say that he, to, is Don's friend.

Rick Chitwood set the wheels turning toward bringing in new jobs when he was working with a contractor from northern Virginia to put a proposal together to submit to the Department of Corrections for building a new prison.

Rick approached the Tazewell County Board of Supervisors led, at that time, by Bill Rasnick for approval to present a request that Tazewell County be considered as a site for the construction of a new prison. When approval was given he continued his quest for a prison.

Rick knew there was land available near the Town of Pocahontas and the thought occurred to him that there might be a possibility of building a new prison in Tazewell County. On a snowy day during the winter, Rick Chitwood, Jim Thompson, and Pat Hurley former Mayor of the Town of Pocahontas, drove to the office of Gene Johnson, Executive Director of the Department of Corrections, in Richmond.

Bill Peery, Glenn Nash, Jim Ramey, and Don Dunford

During the presentation Rick said Pat Hurley gave one of the most passionate speeches he had ever heard regarding the need for the prison.

Within three weeks of the presentation, the land was toured, the people were met, and the decision was made to build in Tazewell County.

*Rick Chitwood and
Governor George Allen*

In the words of Rick Chitwood, "The only role I had in that was that I was working with this contractor and that they were looking at that. I just wanted to make sure the Supervisors of Tazewell County were aware and had an opportunity to see if they could get one and it worked out. A lot of folks were sitting in the right place at the right time."

According to Don Dunford, Rick Chitwood is absolutely one of the finest promoters that Tazewell County could possibly have. Don has observed him with business people and politicians in Richmond and Rick is always at the forefront promoting Tazewell County. In Don's 40 years of knowing Rick Chitwood, Don has found him to only believe in doing what is right. There are those who always try to find out a way not to do something. Rick is an individual who always tries to find out a way to accomplish something. If Tazewell County had more Rick Chitwoods, it would be a better place to live and certainly would be more progressive.

One of Don's fondest memories occurred at the Tazewell Baptist Church when Rick's daughter, Jessica, about 5 years old, became of the centerpiece of the church elections. Don wasn't present at the time but Rick told him that the church members were nominating people for the position of deacon when Jessica proudly stood up and shouted, "Vote for Dun Dunford" who did not attend that church. She had overheard conversations and a catchy radio tune telling the voters of Tazewell County to vote for Don Dunford.

Rick Chitwood's granddaughter, Ella Grace, recognizes Don Dunford as her "Uncle Don." Don smiles when he talks about Ella Grace, his honorary niece.

*Mrs. Jimmy Ramey and
Ella Grace Ramey*

One of Don's memorable sayings is: Nothing happens until you sell something. He firmly believes that statement. He has lived through it many times.

Don Dunford was honored in 2013 by being inducted into the Tazewell High School Hall of Fame.

I reviewed the nomination form and discovered that Don Dunford could have been nominated under several different categories including:

> Business Leader
> Community Volunteer
> Male Athlete
> Elected Official
> Lifetime Achievement
> Philanthropist

There was another category: Other Not Listed – I'm sure he had more attributes that could be listed under that heading.

He was quite honored to be included with the other inductees: Jack Hawks, Robert Marrs, Don Lee, and Dr. James Peery and to be recognized by the Tazewell High School community as a member of the Hall of Fame.

In 2014, Don Dunford was named a Paul Harris Fellow by the Tazewell Rotary Club.

"Never in my wildest dreams would I ever think of being bestowed such an honor – being names a Paul Harris Fellow."

Upon receiving the award Don was speechless as well as a little teary-eyed.

"The Rotary Club is such a prestigious international organization. Being a part of such a program was simply overwhelming."

Don and Nancy

The quotes above were taken from a letter to Fred Harman thanking the Tazewell Rotary for such a fine distinction. The letter expressed the gratitude that he felt toward such an honor as it was bestowed on him, Don Dunford.

CHAPTER 1

WHO IS DON DUNFORD...

If you climb to the top of One-way Mountain and look down into Thompson Valley below, you will see a scene of unexpected beauty and peace. Prettier than a picture postcard, the scene seems to beckon you to stay a while longer and absorb it more fully.

This is where Don Dunford began, and it is here that he always returns. Even though he has come a long way from mowing the hayfields on these mountains, they are still very much a part of his life and always will be. Now, he is a very successful businessman and a retired member of the Virginia House of Delegates for Russell, Buchanan, and Tazewell Counties.

"Who is Don Dunford?" you might ask.

After much research and many conversations, you need to pull up a chair and let me tell you the story of Don Dunford.

Don Dunford at Dunfordtown - Age 2.

He was born on June 15, 1936, and named Charles Donald Dunford. The Charles is obviously for his father, Charles William Dunford; the Donald, well, he isn't very sure where that one came from. Nevertheless, he was called Don, for economy sake, so to speak.

His first home was in Dunfordtown, appropriately enough. It is in Dry Fork near the West Virginia border on the north side of Tazewell County. The town was a mining camp started by Thomas D. Dunford, Don's grandfather, about 1934.

The mine had been operating for some time, but the men needed housing. Seizing an opportunity, Thomas Dunford took the land that he had traded for and began to build on it. Cutting timber from the mountains for framework and buying flooring, windows, doors, and tin for the roof; it only cost about four or five hundred dollars to build a four or five room house.

Dunfordtown was born.

As along as we are on history, perhaps we should take a look at the history of Tazewell County.

The name has a rich history all of its own. It was given by Henry Tazewell, a member of the Virginia House of Burgesses; the Virginia House of Delegates; and of the committee that drew up the Constitution of Virginia in 1776. He was Judge of the District Court and Court of Appeals and a United States Senator from 1794 to 1799.

The county was formed in 1799 from parts of Wythe and Russell Counties. The original area of Tazewell was some three thousand square miles. Its present area is five hundred and twenty-two square miles. Much of the original territory was given to neighboring counties in Virginia and West Virginia.

Tazewell County was frequented by hunters and surveyors long before the first settlers arrived, predominately Scotch-Irish, English, and German descent.

The first pioneer settler in Tazewell was Mathias Harman, Sr., whose father Heinrich Adam Harman had come to America from Germany about 1730. Mathias was born in Strasbourg, Virginia, in 1736. He became an Indian scout, rescuing white settlers taken captive by the Indians. He led an illustrious career and died at Dry Fork in 1832, near where Dunfordtown was later formed. Mathias Harman, Sr. was Don's great-great-great-grandfather; therefore Don is a member of the SAR (Sons of the American Revolution) permitting his daughter Donna to become a member of the DAR (Daughters of the American Revolution).

Tazewell's elevation from the valley floor is 1,900 to 2,700 feet and the mountains are from 2,500 to 4,700 feet. According to the 1980 census, the population of Tazewell was 50,511. Mining and manufacturing are the largest employers in the county with agriculture and wholesale/retail trade close behind.

As far as sheer beauty is concerned, Tazewell County is hard to beat. Gentle rolling pasture lands, green hills and valleys, and clean, clear air as far as the eye can see are the really outstanding commodities of Tazewell. The mountains create a climate seldom uncomfortable in the summer but often treacherous in the winter when snow falls. Warmth and friendliness are the words to describe the inhabitants, also. Even a stranger is made to feel welcome and at home at first meeting. One can only hope that as Tazewell progresses; these qualities will not be tampered with.

The history lesson is over, let's move on.

Charles Dunford, Don's father, was a coal miner and farmer for most of his life. He met Clara Mae Cordle while he was taking a wagon load of corn to the mill in Cedar Bluff. Clara lived just a half mile from the mill on College Hill. Charles wooed her and won her. They were married when Clara was fifteen and Charles was twenty-six.

Don Dunford's Great Grandfather's farm at
Pea Patch - Logs still inside.

Charles & Clara Dunford
1937

Clara was well prepared for a home and family. Her mother had died in childbirth when Clara was only nine years old, leaving her to raise a new baby and a two year old brother. With a ready made family, the couple began life together.

Charles went to work in the coal mines in Amonate because that was the only work to be had.

"The good old days the people talk about today – I don't call them so good. People are living better in our nation today than anywhere in the world," said Charles with a shake of his head to emphasize his point.

On June 15, 1936, Don Dunford was born. His father was working in the face of Number 33 Mine loading coal. When word reached him that he was the proud father of twin boys, he ran the mile's distance from the face of the mine to the outside in record time. There were conflicting stories as to whether he was relieved or disappointed to find that there was only one son, but one can be sure that someone at the mine certainly heard about it. Don, nevertheless, managed to make up for being only one.

Don's mother was the boss of the family, as far as the children were concerned, leaving only the heavy reprimands to their father. One of those heavy reprimands occurred when Don received his first "whipping".

His father had had a flat tire on his car and the process of fixing the flat so fascinated Don that he decided to really give his father something to fix. So – finding several rusty nails, he very methodically put one in front and in back of each tire. Needless to say, his father was displeased with the result.

The willow tree in the front yard was soon minus a branch and little Don was minus the pleasure of sitting for a while.

That was his first lesson, "Always do what's right."

It causes him to believe beyond a shadow of a doubt that his father possessed more honesty and integrity than any man he's ever known. Not to mention that his father swung a pretty mean willow branch!

Another early lesson came from Rhea Moore who ran the Tazewell Farm Bureau. Don and his mother went into the store one day where he saw many things of interest to a small child that only money could buy.

"Mr. Moore, could I have a job working for you?" asked Don.

Mr. Moore looked at the youngster, sizing him up.

"Yes, I need someone to stack the boxes of Jello with all the reds together, all the greens, and all the yellows together in separate stacks."

Mr. Moore knew the task was not as easy as it appeared for a boy who could not read. Red Jello also had green and yellow colors on the boxes as did the green and yellow Jello. The result of Don's best efforts turned out to be quite a hodge-podge of colors.

Proudly Don came out to ask, "Mr. Moore, I would like to be paid now."

"Well, Don, how much do I owe you," asked Mr. Moore.

"One hundred dollars," Don replied.

A quite surprised Mr. Moore went back to see what was so expensive. He found the Jello in various color combinations neatly stacked. Considering the job and the boy, Mr. Moore handed Don ten cents. The little boy walked away happy and never spent the hard earned dime.

The lesson: Never undersell yourself.

When he was seven, Don's father bought a small farm in Thompson Valley, a beautiful agricultural area located between the Clinch and Rich Mountains. Thompson Valley got its name from the Thompsons who, at one time, owned the major portion of the land. William Thompson was one of Tazewell's earliest settlers.

Farm life was great for Don. He hoed corn, not because he wanted to, but because it was a rule of the house. Everyone pulled his or her (Don now had three sisters: Nancy, Peggy, and Dorothy) weight. He milked the cows, fed the hogs, and learned a lot about life.

Don Dunford with sisters, Nancy, Dorothy, Peggy & his daughter, Donna.

One of the best things that ever happened in Don's young life was when his grandfather, Thomas, brought him the ugliest, mangiest, long haired colt. His work was cut out for him, but through constant grooming and a lot of love, Blaze became a beautiful horse and a good friend. She and Don spent many a long afternoon together in the freedom of the valley.

Sundays were always good days on the farm. Don's father still mined coal twelve hours a day and six days a week. The only day they saw each other was Sunday. In the morning they would all walk to the Glenwood Methodist Church, about a mile from home, unless Preacher Boyd happened along to give them a ride.

Sunday dinners were big and usually shared with company. There was fried chicken, gravy, vegetables from the garden, and "kinfolks" galore. Everyone would sit around relaxing, resting, and catching up on the news.

Of course, the men would gather around a battery operated radio to listen to Gabriel Heater and Lowell Thomas talk about a war somewhere in Europe. At age seven, Don knew there was a war, but with all the fascinating things going on in his own backyard, who could think about something that was half way across the globe.

A real turning point in Don's life was starting school.

Don Dunford - First Grader.

"He was a happy-go-lucky boy, never taking anything too seriously. He had lots of ability but he had too much fun to apply himself," Mrs. Stella Ireson, his first grade teacher, said of Don.

First grade was a trying experience for Don.

On a farm, you got up at daybreak and went to bed at whatever hour the chickens roosted. The day was for working and the night was for sleeping. That was what Don was taught.

At school, his first and only whipping came from his refusal to take an afternoon nap. A day nap was something that shoved against everything he had been taught up to that point.

"Don was a likeable child, never in any real trouble. He was just adventurous and very lucky," added Mrs. Ireson.

The arrival of the fourth grade brought with it a new lease on life for Don. He went from a little boy with no goals or purposes more then experiencing everything life had to offer, to a boy with a dream.

Don began to study history; the founding fathers, the House of Burgesses, the beginning of a great nation. He decided he wanted to be a part of it all at that time. It set him on a course from which he was never to waiver.

His teachers agree that Don was always a well liked boy, able to make friends easily.

"He was a bit over fond of talking, but I didn't mind that much," said his government teacher, Mrs. Gladys Hubbard at Tazewell High School. "I enjoyed his discussions and debates in my classes and considered him a real friend. He wasn't the most brilliant student but I knew he would do well. In fact, he always had more PQ than IQ."

Mrs. Hubbard explains that PQ is personality quotient and IQ is intelligence quotient.

"One of the things I liked most about him was his inability to hold a grudge," Mrs. Hubbard continues.

"The best way to do away with enemies is to make friends of them," was what Don told me one day in explanation of how he handled his enemies.

"I wasn't surprised by his declaration in high school that he would someday run for office. He made that statement to me after I told him that evil will persist as long as good men stand idly by and do nothing," said Mrs. Hubbard.

CHAPTER 2

"REAL" FARM LIFE...

Life on the farm was not easy. There was never very much money, even with his father working in the mines. There was always plenty of food and clothing, but not much extra money for luxuries other than an occasional movie or the like. There were no vacations or pleasure trips. They did very little visiting. Most people came to see them.

Don's father was all business; no horseplay. He believed in working fifteen hours a day, seven days a week.

"Man was put on this earth to work and not to play," his father told him.

Don's father was one of the most generous and helpful people he ever knew. He lived his religion. He would do whatever he could to help his neighbors when they needed it.

Don's mother was a good and loving person. She was totally dedicated to her family. She had a sincere desire to make them happy and keep them healthy. She pushed her sometimes lackadaisical son to make sure that he utilized the potential she and the teachers knew he had.

In 1948, Mrs. Dunford became ill with chronic bronchitis. On the advice of Dr. Mary Elizabeth Johnson, the family made a trip by car to Mesa, Arizona, right outside of Phoenix.

There the young family from the mountains of Virginia lived on a western ranch. Don's father worked as ranch hand, planting cotton, sorghum grain, irrigating, and cultivating. It was hard but very interesting work and play for the whole family.

Don finished the fifth grade in Mesa receiving as much education in books as he did in rodeos and real cowboys.

During the summer the children worked chopping cotton and trimming the Johnson grass from the irrigation ditches. The owner of the ranch paid them three dollars for every one hundred pounds of cotton, which was pretty good money as far as they were concerned. They were used to working for nothing!

In the fall, Don started the sixth grade. Due to Arizona's testing program, he was moved into the seventh grade because he was further along in his studies than the Arizona children. His sister, Peggy, was also moved ahead.

The coming of Christmas and Mrs. Dunford's improved health made the family homesick. In January of 1949, the Dunford's packed up the car and returned to Thompson Valley. The teachers said that the children's advanced grades were perfectly suitable, so, with memories of Wild West roundups, life went on.

Mr. Dunford decided not to go back to the mines. In the fifteen years he had worked in them he had seen too many men die and become disabled.

"I could work in the mines another five years and be dead, or quit and live another thirty or forty years," he told his family.

He took the obvious choice and moved the family two miles up the creek in Thompson Valley to a "real farm" of three hundred fifty acres.

Farming became his full time profession. Mr. Dunford built a new home with something they were not heretofore used to – electricity and indoor plumbing.

It fascinated Don. He had only seen it in town and at school. After a gas powered washer and a battery operated radio, it was a definite thrill.

Don, Dorothy, Peggy, & Nancy on Don's 12th Birthday in Higley, Arizona.

Farm life became "real" farm life. The Dunfords now had a herd of cows and sheep added to the chickens and hogs. Although Don's father didn't believe in tractors and used a horse team instead to do the plowing, they managed to do very well.

The ten long hours a day in the hay fields in the summer were to prove very helpful to Don in the future; but, in the present, Don was discovering a myriad of new things, other than electricity.

The beginning of high school opened many doors for him. Girls no longer meant his three little sisters. Now – they were very interesting. It was another truly "fascinating experience" making the transition from child to bonafide teenager.

His next discovery was football. He had never seen it before until the summer preceding his sophomore year. Don had always looked up to and played with the older boys in school. Bill Peery and the others didn't seem to mind because Don gave his all to whatever he did. When the older boys began to play football, Don began to play also.

He's not sure now whether it was his love of the game or his desire to get out of the hay fields that made him tryout for the team; but nevertheless, he made it. He started his first year on the bench of the varsity team.

Don had always been involved in things. He had been part of various plays, such as the classic "Don't Steal My Penny" and many others. He had been in the all state chorus and glee club and he was active in vocational agriculture programs. His activities had to be limited to allow Don to do his chores around the farm; but somehow, football won out and Don was excused from his chores to play the game.

Picture Post Card of Tazewell when Don Dunford was in High School.

His freshman year in high school introduced him to the equations and theorems of geometry that he loved. He looked at them as pieces of a puzzle and loved the way they worked together.

Don found football to be as good a preparation as anything for future life. It was not very different from running and jumping up and down the hills at home and not any more strenuous than working on the farm.

Although he sat on the bench most of his first year, he remained dedicated to the team. Bill Peery and Jim Ramey, two of his friends on the team, agree that he was not the best on the team, but that his dedication and enthusiasm made up for it.

The Coach Casto Ramsey had a great influence on Don and the whole team. The Coach taught him to pay the price to be a winner and the value of desire and the

Mr. & Mrs. Casto Ramsey, Don Dunford's Football Coach.

importance of playing the way you practice.

"Football is a contest between two groups of young men in order to ascertain which has the most desire, dedication, greatest capability, and most discipline. It is a good training device for youth," stated Coach Ramsey.

"Anyone can be a winner if they first decide which contest they wish to win and then dedicate themselves to that particular goal or dream. The mistake is to measure success in dollars alone. You can be a success in your field without financial reward," was the message that football taught to Don. These thoughts have kept Don going for some time and probably account in part for his restlessness.

High school did one more thing for Don. It gave him a life long friend in Bill Peery, "Bido" as he is more commonly known. They have shared a great deal of their youth and their adulthood, even though jobs and miles have often separated them for years at a time. They always seem to be able to pick up the pieces and lend a helping hand when needed. Both are equally proud of the other's success, and both are always willing to go that extra mile for the other.

Don Dunford Football Player.

1951 THS "UNDEFEATED" BULLDOGS
COACHES-CASTO RAMSEY & JAMES LAVANCHE

REESE BAILEY	"COKIE" KITTS	DOUG PETERS
BILL BENSON	TERRY KITTS	CHARLES PHILLIPS
FRANKIE BOOTH	GEORGE LEWIS	JAMES RAMEY
WARNER COLLINS	JAY LOCKHART	BILL SLAUGHTER
JOE CRABTREE	DONNIE MANN	BUDDY STEVENSON
DON DUNFORD	BOBBY McGLOTHIN	AMEL STEVENSON
JACK GILLESPIE	GUY McGLOTHIN	BILL STEVENSON
ALBERT HAGY	ROY MORRISON	RICHARD TURNER
CARL HAGY	GLENN NASH	BILL WOODALL
RONDLE HILL	JIMMY ORREN	JOE WRIGHT
RONALD KISER	BILL PEERY	

1951 Tazewell High School "Undefeated" Bulldogs Team Roster.

"If I were to go into battle tomorrow and could chose only one person to go with me, I'd choose Bill Peery," said Don.

"Don is a loose-knit extrovert who is liable to cut loose at any minute," said Bill of his best friend. "He was always an attention getter in school but also a fairly good student. Don is not open with his emotions; but, as a friend if you need him, he'll come through."

Don graduated from high school a year ahead of Bill and went on to college for a year. Bill graduated from high school about the same time Don finished his freshman year and the two decided to join the Marines together. For some reason this idea did not last long and the two changed their plans and headed for Washington, D.C. and a job.

They pounded the pavement for about two weeks, unwilling to admit defeat. They were not having the best of luck finding any kind of job in 1954. Then they finally got jobs parking cars in a lot at the corner of 14th and New York. They were admittedly the best parking lot attendants in Washington, D.C. The glamour of it all soon paled and they packed off for something better.

The two boys had always shared the dream of coaching football someday.

For Bill, the dream came true. He coached at Beaver High School in Bluefield; Emory and Henry College; and then became head football coach at Giles High School in Pearisburg and later, head coach at Richlands High School.

The teamwork continued. Don would go to the opposing teams' games and watch them play. He would then come back and report to Coach Peery any of the weaknesses of the competition. That's how Don earned the nickname of "007".

'No Problems' With
For Vet School Fund

Richmond Bureau

D — Different approaches
ey for a school of veteri-
Virginia Tech pose no
Richard Bagley, chair-
propriations Commit-

ate Don Dunford, D-Tazewell,
time ago introduced a bill providing
illion to get the school cranked up.

en, over the weekend, the Appro-
ns Committee — at the suggestion of
y and Delegate Jerry Geisler, minori-
er in the House — showed its sup-
$1.25 million for a school by a 19-0

e   , Geisler said $700,000 would be
this   ype building.

         year's operations would cost
ored a   e second year's $400,000, he
relief to
inia from
180 days   agley emphasized that if
uction where   e adopted by the com-
involved. The   ir suggestion it would
me legislation   nts for a school as
Assembly last   Council of Higher
vetoed by the
It provides that at   — as the council
ssed days be made up l be a regional
school be concluded on
June 17. The bill   he Bagley-
funding shall   the gover-
         school   e ad-

nor authority to see that all
quirements are met.

The Bagley-Geisler ar
doubtedly will be approved
sures Tech of a vet school
pushed so hard here by a nu
tors and so strongly suppor
the state by numerous fa
groups.

Dr. William Lavery, pre
said the school could be re
first class in the fall of 1980.

While Virginia legisla
whelmingly in favor of th
about school, Maryland and
have indicated willingness to
gional venture.

Legislation has been intr
states that puts them on rec
the establishment of a school

And steps have been t
legislation under consideratio
to make sure that Virginia
funds for the school.

Private funds have been

At a news conference la
ers of the Virginia Farm B
tion and other groups tha
school say they are prepare
million in private funds for t

At the same time, the r
said the institution will cost
lion.

CHAPTER 3

A YOUNG MAN WITH PLANS...

In 1953, Don went to Virginia Polytechnic Institute to study animal husbandry. He wanted to be a veterinarian.

Knowing the situation at home, he applied for a scholarship from Sears while he was still in high school. The competition consisted of a form to be filled out and a short essay to be written on why the scholarship should be awarded to him, or something like that. Being a good one with words, Don won the scholarship. The only drawback was that it was only

Don Dunford - Cadet.

for one year. His father assured him that he would help all he could.

All students (VPI was a men's college) were required to join the corps of cadets and that is where Don got his first taste of military life. Due to the strict regimentation, there was not much excitement on the campus. There weren't many parties or dances; just an occasional water fight in the dorms with every man for himself including the commanding officer, Commander Barnett.

Even with the lack of outside interests, Don was not exactly a model student. He did well in history and math, his main points of interest. He managed to flunk English 101 in three consecutive quarters because his professor was unable to stimulate him.

"You can't learn English," said his professor.

"You can't teach English," Don promptly responded.

One important thing about Don Dunford is that he says exactly what he thinks regardless of the circumstances.

The year at VPI confirmed his feelings about math, history, and government. He also saw that perhaps a long-term education, such as one required to become a veterinarian, was not going to be possible for him, at that time.

Farming had been bad that year. Livestock prices hit rock bottom and there was not much money for higher education in the Dunford family.

Don left VPI and went to work for Armour and Company Meatpackers in Richmond. He told them that he was an old farm boy and wanted to learn the business from the ground up. They took him at his word and put him to work loading trucks.

Don Dunford - USMC.

That lasted a year.

"There is no future in this," he told his family.

He moved on.

He joined the Marines for real. His basic training in that summer of 1956 lasted thirteen weeks and three days at Parris Island, South Carolina, which was notorious for its toughness. One day in Parris Island seemed like a month to Don.

It wasn't long before those ten hour days in the hay fields of Thompson Valley in the summer came home to him that June, July, and August. He was used to the hot sun, the exhaustion of the body and there was no way that the drill instructor could drive him until he dropped because he wouldn't fall. He had had his conditioning as a boy in the hay fields of Thompson Valley. Perhaps that's why he was chosen as section leader for his platoon in boot camp.

Don Dunford - Virginia Tech

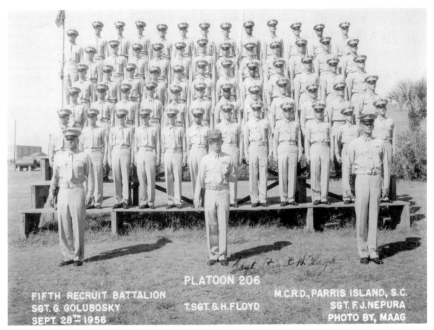

FIFTH RECRUIT BATTALION   M.C.R.D., PARRIS ISLAND, S.C.
SGT. G. GOLUBOSKY   T.SGT. S.H.FLOYD   SGT. F.J.NEPURA
SEPT. 28ᵗ 1956   PHOTO BY, MAAG

Marine Corps Platoon 206 - Parris Island, SC
Don is holding Guide-on as Platoon Leader.

After all this rigorous training, the Marine Corps decided to utilize him at an office job. He was put in charge of Personnel and Classification for H.Q. Company of the Second Shore Party Battalion. His duties were to take requests from various other Marine Corps installations and match the requests with an individual from the Second Shore Party Battalion. In other words, if a request came for a man for guard duty at the brig at the Naval Air Station in Norfolk, for example, he would find a man capable of the assignment and send him on his way.

"I wouldn't take any amount of money for the experience, but no amount of money could make me go through it again!" Don says of his matchmaking days.

Don left the Marines at a time when it was almost impossible to find a job. The country, under Dwight Eisenhower, was at a standstill. With perseverance and an open mind, one could find a job if he looked hard enough.

He couldn't afford to go back to school. His father's farm was not really prospering. Don began to look around for something that he could do.

That's when he saw an advertisement in the Richmond papers for police officers for the Richmond Bureau of Police. With his experience in the Marines, he knew he could handle just about anything. With his interest in law, and the thought of making new laws, he would try his hand at upholding the present laws.

It was a challenge.

He applied and was hired.

He reported to the Police Academy at the Mosque in Richmond where he was sworn in as a patrolman on the Richmond Police Force. This ceremony would be remembered during another swearing in ceremony a little further downtown in the State Capitol a few years later.

"The training was excellent," says Don. "The officers were trained in the law, the use of firearms and how to handle themselves in just about any situation they might encounter on the street."

The young patrolman found it all fascinating and, like everything else he did, he threw himself into it completely.

Colonel Frank Duling, who at the time Don was on the force was Captain Duling, Commanding Officer, Personnel and Training Division and who later became Chief of Police, says he was impressed with Don from their first meeting.

"He seemed to want to get ahead…and to be proud of police work," said Duling.

They have maintained contact over the years. Colonel Duling even had a copy of Don's service record bound in a red police folder for Don to give to his daughter as a keepsake.

Colonel Duling is sure that Don is the first police officer to go into the House of Delegates and is rightfully proud of that fact.

While Don was still in training, he found many interesting new experiences and things to learn. Things happened fast in Richmond. One day in the classroom, the instructor staged an experiment straight out of a psychology textbook. Through the door in the front of the classroom came a women dressed in the "darndest garb" he had ever seen. Close behind her came a man, also in strange clothing, wearing a mask and shooting a blank pistol. The couple ran through the center of the classroom and out the back door, leaving a speechless group of police cadets.

The lieutenant instructing the class immediately handed out a test composed of forty or fifty questions aimed at identifying the two people and ascertaining the facts about what happened.

Very few of the cadets passed the test. Each had a different impression of the episode, different hair colors, dress colors, numbers of shots fired, and not even the right color of masks. It proved to all of them that you cannot always trust what you see or depend entirely on the word of a witness. The details of a crime or occurrence are not always easily ascertainable.

During Don's training, all of his progress reports were satisfactory or more than satisfactory. His personal appearance, neatness, promptness, and attendance were never less than satisfactory and often more than satisfactory.

Don began his forty-four hour week and career in the police force at $138.00 per week. He was not destined to be rich as a policeman. He was given permission to do off-duty work in uniform and had a part-time job at Sears as a salesman to help supplement his income.

Don Dunford was a young man with plans. At the age of twenty-one, he had his whole life ahead of him.

During his fifteen months on the police force, he spent most of his time in a traffic control car. Although his days were not as exciting as the TV policemen who have two or three shoot-outs a week, Don had his share of excitement.

He investigated many accidents, automobile and others. With his natural feeling for people along with his hometown warmth and friendliness, he was able to handle the not always pleasant situation with a measure of compassion and understanding.

In July of 1958, Don was sent to investigate an accident at a local paper factory that had resulted in the death of an employee. There seemed to be some question as to whether it was caused by another employee. After further investigation by the detective squad, it was deemed an accident with no one at fault.

The president of the company wrote to Don's captain with his impressions:

I wish to take this opportunity to express my appreciation for the courtesy and consideration shown by Patrolman C. D. Dunford who was investigating officer in the recent tragedy in which our employee…was involved.

I consider it to be thoughtful beyond the normal call of duty for Patrolman Dunford to have called…, in the evening, after completing the investigation of the accident, to tell the employee that involuntary manslaughter charges were not going to be preferred against him. This was undoubtedly very comforting to…in this instance.

Again, please accept our thanks and express our appreciation to Patrolman Dunford.

In August of 1958, a more typical traffic accident showed still another side of Don's characteristic way of dealing with people. He had stopped a man who was driving too fast and advised him of his error. The man, who by the way was a doctor, writes this note of appreciation:

> The officer informed me that I was driving too fast under the circumstances, reminded me most courteously of the speed limits, and requested my future cooperation in that regard.
>
> I wish to commend this gentleman upon the complete courtesy of his approach to me. One could not, under the circumstances, wish other than to cooperate to the fullest.
>
> I feel that he is a credit to the Richmond Police Department.

"On most occasions," Don says, "for minor traffic offenses, people appreciate not being arrested or written up, naturally. Having their errors called to their attention and warned, that in itself is a deterrent."

One last letter received from the minister of a local church where Patrolman Dunford had spoken is very complimentary.

> It was our pleasure to have Police Officer Dunford speak to a group of our young people, ages 12 to 15, this past Sunday. It was a pleasure to have him with our group and, in my opinion, he did an excellent job of public relations between the police officer and our group. Our normal meeting time is less than an hour; however, Officer Dunford had young people still questioning him at five minutes to eleven. This indicates that he was successful in stimulating thought among this group.
>
> I have known Officer Dunford for some time now and I am sure he is an asset to our city police force. He is one of the finest young men I have run into in any profession since my arrival in Richmond…

Not only did Don Dunford turn out to be a kind and affable officer, but he also was good press relations for the department.

"The most writhing experience is to arrive on the scene of an accident and find people dead and/or mangled," states Don with a shake of his head for emphasis. "I saw some pretty terrible accidents while on the force. One of the hardest lessons for a policeman to learn is to remain calm and detached in thought and action in order to do the best possible job. Otherwise, he is of no use to anyone."

It sounds a bit cold but as Don explains, "You become conditioned. Blood becomes the aftermath of what happened. You're not responsible for it, only to take care of the situation at hand." Frowning he adds, "You never look forward to it. You just have to accept it as part of the job, but never, never become satisfied with it or say it doesn't make any difference."

Probably one of the things that Don is most proud of in his law enforcement career is his part in the apprehension of a fencing ring.

One night while on the midnight shift in his patrol car, he noticed two young men walking up the street looking in every car and shop window. After watching them for about ten or fifteen minutes, the men went into a restaurant. A short time later, he noticed the same men on another part of the street going through the same procedure. Feeling that it was too early to arrest or charge them with any real crime, he decided to keep an eye on them for another hour or two.

At one point, a car drove up to the two men, stopped, and the two young men were called over for a discussion. After conferring with the two men who were on foot, those in the car circled the block several times very slowly.

Don made his move. He got the license number of the car. He drove through an alley where he caught the two men and charged them with night prowling. He arrested them.

The detective squad followed up on the case, and with the address obtained from the two men, found a number of items in their home that had recently been reported stolen. With the license number, the gang was traced to Baltimore where a complete fencing exchange had been set up between Baltimore and Richmond. Don earned a commendation and a lot pats on the back for his alertness.

The urge to go back to school and find a new goal, a new challenge began to grow. He was now in a position to go back to school and finish his education which he had always wanted to do. Police work had been interesting and rewarding but he was ready for a new challenge.

Don is a people person and dealing with people is one of the things he loves. He is seldom satisfied letting things remain as they are. He had bigger plans ahead.

On January 5, 1959, he turned in his letter of resignation:

> I, Patrolman C.D. Dunford, do hereby submit my resignation, effective January 21, 1959.
>
> My tour of duty in the Richmond Bureau of Police has been most pleasant and my sole reason for resigning is that I may finish my college work. As soon as I complete this objective, I shall return and seek employment once more.

The notation at the bottom of the letter reads: "If Patrolman C.D. Dunford seeks reemployment after finishing schooling noted above in resignation, I recommend that he be rehired."

It was signed by the Captain of the Traffic Safety Division and approved by the Chief of Police and the Director of Public Safety.

Not a bad way to end a career.

CHAPTER 4

DON AND NANCY WERE THROWN TOGETHER A LOT...

Don & Nancy Dunford.

Don chose Concord College just outside of Princeton, West Virginia, as the place to further his education. He had a good reason for choosing Concord. His best friend, Bill Peery, was there. It was Bill, as a matter of fact, who helped convince Don to make the decision to go back to college at that point. Bill had just started back himself in September. With his friend's advice and encouragement and his own desire for more knowledge; there he was.

Concord had once been the state normal school and now was a four year college offering programs of study in the liberal arts, medicine, science, business administration, and teacher training. It was a good school, the tuition was not too high, and the fact that it was just forty-five miles from Tazewell, helped him to make up his mind.

Despite his feelings about police work, Don's old love of mathematics captured him again. The challenge of the puzzle, the theorems, and equations drew him to a different concentration. He decided to major in business and accounting. He had tried and passed Business English at the University of Richmond night school while still on the police force.

He took more interest in his classes now. They were not as tedious as they were before because they were the means to an interesting new end, whatever that may be. He had learned the value of an education. Of course, football was still on the agenda with Don playing on the team. Bill, in the process of studying for his Master's in physical education, heartily approved.

Things were different for the two boys from Tazewell this time. They were men now with differing experiences. In the years since high school, Bill had married Ann and they had a little daughter. There was no more painting the town red for the two of them.

Bill kept his eyes open for the perfect date for Don. Having found someone wonderful in Ann, he wanted his friend to find that someone wonderful also. It goes without saying that Don, like any other single young man of twenty-three was enjoying the matchmaking.

Don often brought his dates to dinner at the Peery's apartment. Ann was never too busy to set an extra place. She was always the perfect hostess and a great cook with "the best homemade chili beans I ever tasted," said Don with a smile.

Bill & Ann Peery.

Even without dates Don was a regular visitor. Bill and Ann were his family away from home. In return, he babysat for their daughter Beth while studying for his classes.

All in all, going back to school proved to be a great experience for Don.

"There is no better life than that in college," Don says.

For Don it was a good life.

"College is that certain environment that can only be experienced by being there and being a part of it all," he adds.

As a member of the Kappa Sigma Kappa Fraternity, he learned the philosophy of one for all and all for one that later "grants the character one needs to become a worthwhile member of the community and participate in its functions."

Don's fraternity had a sister sorority on campus, the Alpha Sigma Tau Sorority. They ate in the cafeteria together and shared parties and dances and such. The girls sewed the letters on the boys' jackets and did other little things, and all had a good time. Together they, more or less, helped each other out.

In the sorority was a girl with whom Don had some marketing and economics classes, by the name of Nancy Bowman. They had one thing in common. Both of their fathers were involved in coal mining. Nancy's father was in a different end of it though. He installed coal mining machinery in West Virginia.

Nancy and Don were thrown together a lot for about a year, neither of them thinking much about it. It was a year before they actually started to date.

One evening Don stopped in at Nancy's dorm to ask if she would sew the letters on his jacket for him. They stood in the lobby and chatted for a while.

"You promised two weeks ago you'd go out with me," he said with his typical impudence in a voice loud enough to be heard by others in the lobby.

"You are mistaken," answered Nancy not knowing what he was talking about or why.

Undaunted, Don kept it up until a mortified Nancy got her coat and went with him.

It was not a very romantic beginning but it did lead to sporadic dating and a friendship and respect that is still strong for both of them today.

When Nancy graduated in 1961, her father and mother were going to Phoenix, Arizona, to live. Nancy went with them. She and Don kept in touch through the mail while she was gone, and he continued to study accounting.

When he felt that he had all the courses he needed, he decided to leave Concord. He thought about going back to the police force but the excitement of a new career challenged him and changed his mind.

In 1961, Don went to work for Armour and Company Meatpackers again; but this time, as a salesman in the Food Services Division in Charlotte, North Carolina.

He did well and enjoyed the work; so much so that in 1962, he was transferred to the Armour Plant in Durham, North Carolina, as head of the Food Services Division.

That same year, Nancy and her family came back to West Virginia from Phoenix. They began seeing each other again, a bit more seriously this time.

The final step towards marriage came at Nancy's cousin's wedding when a teasing relative asked, "When are you two going to tie the knot?"

Dear Wife - Nancy Dunford.

The subject was broached and they decided to set the date.

Don and Nancy were married in August of 1962.

It is said that behind every great man is a great lady. In Don's own words, this is true of him and Nancy. All who knew Don before he married say that Nancy has been a good influence on him. She has managed to take out the wild and reckless side of his nature and to encourage his better qualities and stability. She is critical of his business and political activities in the way any partner or friend would be. She continues to stand tall behind him in all of his decisions.

"Ours is not a clinging vine relationship. We have conferences on business dealings and whenever Don is going to make a big move, I am in the discussion and planning," said Nancy.

He depends on her knowledge as an accountant and practical level-headed advisor.

Both of them are complete, self-sufficient individuals when they are away from each other.

Nancy felt the unfairness of men's wages being higher than hers while she worked in the trust department of a bank in North Carolina. In order to equalize things, she went back to school, Duke University, to become a teacher, where she knew she would be paid fairly.

Nancy loved teaching and seeing the light in the children's eyes when they begin to understand.

They always have something new and interesting to say.

She was also involved in adult education which she liked best of all because the students were so eager to learn.

Nancy found herself learning right along with them.

The couple lived in an apartment in Durham right over their landlord, Roy Smith. Roy and Don became great buddies. They played golf together as often as possible and watched football games.

Little by little through their long talks, Roy began to impress on Don how lucrative the building business was; especially rental property. Unwittingly, he planted a seed in Don's mind that would someday blossom into a bumper crop of ingenuity and success.

Don began to feel the need for new challenges having gone about as far at Armour as he wanted to go. Don was and is a very restless person who is never satisfied with the status quo. It is not reckless restlessness. He is a person who needs constant challenge and stimulation for what he is doing. Once he has met a particular goal or challenge, he is not happy until he is striving for another one.

In February, 1964, he went to work at Valleydale Meatpackers in Salem, Virginia, and proceeded to design and set up a food services department and a beef fabrication department also. When this challenge was met and working, the old restlessness took hold of him again.

On a weekend trip to Tazewell, they passed a little country store that was going out of business. Don is a great believer in the free enterprise system and in the theory of everyone helping themselves as much as they can. He especially likes to be on his own and free to do what he thinks is best. He feels that most big businesses stifle their employee's natural initiative and innovative thinking.

"If an employee wants to get along, he has to go along," says Don. "People have more to offer than to function as a machine."

Don had been involved with this type of thinking for four years and the store offered a welcomed change. He'd be his own boss and he'd be in Tazewell.

In May, 1965, he leased the store building and the Thompson Valley Grocery and Service Center opened its door under the sole proprietorship of Don and Nancy Dunford.

His first bit of "innovative thinking" was evidenced when he put up a sign at the entrance to Thompson Valley:

THE THOMPSON VALLEY GROCERY AND SERVICE CENTER
WELCOMES YOU TO BEAUTIFUL THOMPSON VALLEY

The store proved to be a success, especially for someone who knew nothing about the retail business.

His enthusiasm and willingness to learn plus the faith and encouragement of his wife and friends helped to turn the store into a thriving business.

There were some early problems. Don needed a loan shortly after the store opened. When he went to the Bank of Tazewell County, Ray Dodson assured him that he could have the loan if his father would cosign it.

Don sat back and said, "Mr. Dodson, I'm sure that my father would sign for the loan, but I am a grown man, on my own, and I will not ask him to sign it."

Don stood up to leave.

Ray Dodson asked Don to wait a minute while he checked with Walter Baugh who happened to know Don.

"Can we lend Don Dunford money on his signature alone?" Ray Dodson asked Walter Baugh.

"Yes!" Walter Baugh answered emphatically.

Don had his loan.

Because of the fact that it was given to him on faith, he worked a little harder to pay it back.

"What it takes to start your own business," philosophizes Don, "is blood, guts, and credit."

By 1968, the store was well on its way and Don and Nancy discovered they were a little ahead of the game. When their daughter, Donna Elaine, was two and Nancy was no longer teaching, Don decided to take his old friend Roy Smith's advice and start building.

His first project was an apartment building to be leased.

That same year, Don sold the country store and started a wholesale and retail tire store, the Mohawk Tire Sales. In fact, Don spent many evenings in Akron Ohio dining with officials of Mohawk Tire and Rubber Company trying to persuade them to build a factory in Tazewell County. They instead built in Salem, Virginia. He continued to delve into business, finding his first apartment building a relative success. Nancy kept books for the tire store and acted as a kind of secretary. Soon the tire business was also a success.

In 1973, he broadened his ambitions and built the first shopping center of Tazewell. It was called the Four-Way Shopping Plaza. It included his tire business, a supermarket, and various other concerns.

Today there are twenty-three businesses in the plaza. Don's dreams were beginning to come true and with the coming of affluence he began to think more seriously about the needs of his community instead of his own and those of his family.

In 1976, Don began looking for a new challenge, one that would fill a need.

Tazewell County has always had two newspapers, weekly newspapers. One was geared towards Richlands and one was more for the Bluefield area. There was no paper that covered the whole county. On

Don Dunford.

his way to Richmond one day, Don began thinking about this and decided that a paper that covered the whole county would certainly be a worthwhile contribution.

He formed a corporation, with himself as president, and the Tazewell County Free Press was born. As the name suggested, it was a free paper of about twelve pages that spoke to the entire county every week.

There was still another gap in Tazewell's community that bothered Don. The only movie theater was a drive-in that catered mainly to the younger crowd. With his friends in mind, he started building a twin cinema right behind his shopping center. It opened on June 29, 1978. He managed it himself in order to keep control of the kind of movies shown. He wouldn't allow X-rated movies on his screens.

"I just couldn't do that to my friends," he says. Being a new theatre owner I joined NATO, The National Association of Theatre Owners. I was invited to the National Convention in New Orleans and participated as a guest speaker. My address was "My Life as a New Small Town Theatre Owner." Great Experience, while I was there I had dinner with Bert Reynolds and Dolly Parton. They were in the midst of filming "The Best Little Whore House in Texas."

Don has never forgotten where he came from and how it felt to be there. He is generous almost to a fault in the community, with his friends, and with his church. He is equally as generous with his time and advice as with his affluence.

Digging around in his past revealed to me a question he had been asked about what he thought of himself and his success, he answers:

"I have felt mostly dissatisfaction. I'm always looking for another bridge to cross and another mountain to climb. I have always wanted to make a mark, to make a meaningful contribution to make this a better place to live. I'm proud of what I've done in the community, with my life and in politics; but, I can't shake the feeling that there is something else to be done."

That was why politics was right for him. He was never satisfied with things being just good enough or all right. They must be great.

CHAPTER 5

WORDS FROM LOIS SWEETSER...

Lois Sweetser.

The Dunford garden is out my front window, across the lawn, over the road, in the foreground of Dial Rock. Here is a view of peaceful freedom, beauty, and contentment. The family members, who are come-and-go components in this live pastoral picture, add to the feeling and joy of the panoramic scene. I pause sometimes to look awhile.

Early one summer evening when the welcomed rain had ceased, I was checking the goings on in the neighborhood through my window panes. Situated in the mud between rows of beans and corn stood Don in a tuxedo. Such a contrast was at once humorous, but moreover, I immediately recognized this glimpse as symbolic. Don's polished ways are intercepted by his down-to-earth nature occasionally. It's this combination that makes him attractive and fascinating. When he moves in high places and concentrates on important matters, his wisdom is evidenced by his practical and versatile earlier experiences.

Two obvious traits, both magnetic, are his delight in humor and his sensitivity toward people. These were the demonstrative qualities I noticed first in the neighbor I would soon learn to admire for many more reasons. My first day in town, we met, at noontime, at the Martingale.

"You folks new in town?" he asked and then introduced himself and Nancy. His easy smile and well-groomed appearance made him likeable right away. Meeting this friendly couple was our social preamble to Tazewell. Later that first day when we bought a house and asked about the vicinity we learned that they were just across the street. We were pleased.

He was the first one to come calling, but we had been in town about a month before we knew he was the distinguished representative to the House of Delegates from the Third District.

New friends implied only that he was "running".

"He has an important visitor," we said when we saw the low numbered license plate on a good looking car in his driveway.

We were flattered that he frequently dropped in to get acquainted and to clue us in on things one needs and likes to know about a new community. He sat on my kitchen stool, sampled cookies, and told me how he had planned since fourth grade to become a legislator. He was entertaining and educational.

We sat by their pool and enjoyed getting to know their household that summer. I remember an evening when the full moon arrived from behind Buckhorn Mountain while we visited on the patio. Its course without our vision effectuated a mood of special grace. We absorbed the cool breezes coming through our valley and indulged in the desserts Nancy brought from her pretty and completely equipped kitchen. From the few swimmers came mirthful noises. They splashed and panted and yelped! The clumps of planted flowers, in the night time shadows, looked romantic. I thought – this is perfect.

Sometimes an invitation comes via tractor and its driver up the two hundred feet stretch of the hill.

"Come right down. We've got some homemade ice cream," or "we'll be cutting a watermelon," shouts Don over the tractor noise.

Don and Nancy are both excellent story tellers. They are good laughers. Donna has the same zest but more than anything, I guess swimming rates tops with her. Edna Bowman's graciousness has a penetrating influence over this household.

"That's Nancy's mom," Don exclaimed as he glanced toward Edna Bowman with tenderness when we first were introduced to her.

Scooter, Donna's canine friend, is the most mischievous of all who live there. His name is thus because Donna and her dad thought it to be descriptive of his behavior when he first arrived. The pudgy form and dashing movements implied the enduring title.

Felix and Fudgie are the cats whose function it seems is to stand guard over the premises from their perch atop a parked vehicle.

Don and Tazewell are synonymous. Everywhere we go – early morning and at night – Don is there or he is mentioned.

"Do you think there is only one Don Dunford?" I eventually asked.

People smile when you say his name. In no small part has his humor contributed to his success.

"Can't help but like Don," is a popular slogan among people I know.

"Ya gotta get up in the morning," and "I like a hustler." I've heard him give that advice to someone who was pursuing success. He lives by these standards and he expects it in others. He admires this. Here is a man who belongs to the past, the present, and to many new beginnings.

His work ethic theory and his sense of responsibility were also staunch approaches to accomplishment by former generations. The habit of visiting around the neighborhood is an old custom. Sharing his things in a real spirit of generosity and friendliness is an attitude not often practiced these days in which we do our living. Don remains true to these ideas. His alert, vital characteristics keep him in the hub of our world today.

In many little towns like Tazewell he has an influential role.

Beyond, in Richmond, we know he maintains respect because of his concerns and willingness to persevere. State-wide newspapers frequently report his vigor. Colleagues and acquaintances, alike, listen to him. On voting day, back home, the constituency convinces their Delegate he's right for them.

He's not afraid of the difficult. Compassion, an ever present trait, determines largely the credibility of this one. I feel encouraged for our well being with Don as our representative.

"I believe with his other supports, that he is really smart! The future is his business."

He stated, "This (politics) is my life."

Legislative committee assignments and his leadership on commissions, prove his involvement in what is yet to be. He is an instrument to bring about subsequent days of merit for first, his own Donna, the community, Virginia, and the entire country. Don's hopes and expectations are conspicuous in his everyday conversations – socially or in business situations. His openness is one of his best features; he is a comfortable conversationalist. Since enthusiasm and impulsiveness are forces in his personality, my guess would be that a positive outlook coupled with patience has been a matter of cultivation. Polite manners are a smooth ingredient in his life style, except for the time he arrived late for Sunday School eating a donut and didn't have any for the rest of us.

A complete expose about Don must essentially include his affiliation with the church. He told me he has always felt a loyalty.

I have known him to teach Sunday School and to be the Lay Member of the Main Street United Methodist Church to the Annual Conference and to serve in many capacities in between. Church members recognize him as a leader who is generous with his time and money. His faithfulness is demonstrated whenever he has the opportunity to invite others to worship, and again as he contemplatively performs in the various missions of the church. His role as a Christian witness is seen in all areas of his life.

I submit him as a good example.

Ours, the Matt S. Martin Sunday School Class placed a Bible in his newly redecorated office in Richmond. This was done in recognition and in support of his high values. It makes a difference when he's at Sunday School. Theology, mixed with his wit and directness is refreshing, always. Don and Nancy entertain the class and their families twice during the summer. Everybody likes to go.

The Lions move in once a year for a steak supper. Nancy and Edna put on an enormous feed and I've heard it related as a highlight of the club year.

Neighbors are at liberty to use their pool all season – such steady hospitality is surely a rarity. This munificence is typical. The Dunfords are noted for their unsparing deeds. Don has just the right tool someone needs to make a repair. Where you can get the hard to find, Don knows. If he sees your bush needs pruning, he does it.

When he deemed our garden needed cultivation, he came with his rototiller and conducted the job. Before we moved to town, he prepared a vegetable garden for us. He plowed. Nancy and Bonnie Sisk dropped the seeds, and we were the pleased recipients of a welcoming gift. Their thoughtfulness continued. They lugged produce from their gardens while ours was maturing.

Some domestic statistics are these. I'll tell the kinds of things he likes to eat – onions, applesauce, white fudge, jelly, Nancy's coconut cream pie, and Edna's special three-layer, homemade, fresh coconut cake. All should know this – whereas Don wants company, he also wishes them to make an appropriate departure. He turns in for the day at a reasonable hour to rise early in the morning time to get propelling. It is a sound habit important to his stamina, apparently. He likes nice clothes; he is precise in his attire. I think his favorite color is blue. He is truly family oriented and it appears these factors sustain equilibrium in his expeditious business world. I marvel at the extent of his attention to private matters. He enjoys a really special harmonious relationship with his own family, his in-laws, his precious Donna, and Nancy, his helpmate and love.

Swimming is for fun as well as for a measure of healthy exercise. Relaxation can be football. Over at Virginia Polytechnic Institute and State University, with the crowd, he roots – or stretched out in bed watching the screen, he likes the suspense of the game. His fall social schedule includes joining the spectators when the local high school team is on the field.

He recalled a story about himself. It happened at a football game and it typifies how habitually he is accepted anywhere. It's the work of his neighborly stance, I think, or maybe his big blue eyes, but he seems to instantly become all right with everybody. Up ahead in the hurrying stadium crowd he noticed a familiar face. He hadn't seen this woman friend for several years and so he dashed, exuberantly, to greet her. From behind, he hurled his arms around her and deposited a kiss on his cheek. When she recovered from the surprise and he explained his mistake in identity, she told him, "That's all right!"

Dunford oppose cut in benefits

Delegate C.D. (Don) Dunford, Tazewell has said that he will oppose projected recommendation by a Virginia Supplemental Retirement System Study Commission to cut or alter retirement benefits for Virginia state employees.

Dunford said that the present VSRS Plan is fair and equitable, and that it should not be tampered with.

He further said that State employees, many of whom have worked a lifetime looking foward to retirement, and then with alterations would not have the benefits they had looked forward to.

Assembly Action

RICHMOND (AP) — These were the [hi]ghts Friday in the Virginia General [Asse]nbly:

A bill was introduced to keep Bland [Coun]ty from having to forfeit $109,000 in lo[cal s]chool funds to the state. Bland was [too] much short in local support for schools [for] "quality education" standards. The [bill] would allow county officials to spend [the] money in the Bland County school sys[tem] over a four year period. Sponsors of [the bi]ll said other counties have been given [the a]lternative in the past.

[Th]e Virginia Senate and House of Dele[gates] passed the first bills of the 1978 Gen[eral] Assembly session. One in the House [would] permit motorists to use studded [snow] tires from Oct. 15 to April 15. A bill [passe]d by the Senate would prohibit insur[ance] companies from refusing to issue or [renew] automobile policies simply because [a vehi]cle is over 10 years old.

The House of Delegates also passed [a bill] that would give a new charter to [Abing]don. The bill makes the first changes [in the] charter since Abingdon was founded [200 y]ears ago.

Sen. Edward Holland, D-Arlington, [said t]he Virginia Senate it's time to stop

picking on the Metro rail system and realize it's a valuable asset to the entire state.

A joint legislative subcommittee recommended that doctors and lawyers stay out of the adoption business and leave it to duly regulated child placement agencies.

Legislation was introduced in the House by Delegate Don Dunford, D-Tazewell, and 73 co-patrons to establish a school of veterinary medicine at Virginia Tech.

Attorney General J. Marshall Coleman had a bill introduced in the Senate to provide uniform sentencing of convicted criminals and abolish the parole system in Virginia.

The Virginia Council of Independent Colleges asked legislators at a hearing on the proposed $9.1 billion state budget to double the individual tuition grants available to students attending private colleges and universities in the state.

A bill was submitted in the House to require the state to license and regulate motor vehicle repair shops. The license could be suspended or revoked if the licensee was found guilty of offenses such as false or misleading advertising, repeated negligence in repair work or misrepresent[ing the cost of repairs]

CHAPTER 6

DON'S WORDS: AN HONOR EVERY CITIZEN SHOULD HAVE...

If I had won the election the first time I ran for public office in 1967, I would not have been able to afford to serve. This is a sad fact, but true one. I was a small businessman in one of the most remote areas of Virginia. At that time, it took a full day to get to and from the state capitol in Richmond. I could not afford the travel time and the time in Richmond away from my business to fulfill my duties as a state legislator. This factor affects every Virginia politician, and those who wish to seek office.

Virginia's General Assembly is composed of "citizen legislators." It is not a full time functioning body of professionals, but is still guided by the principles set forth by our founding fathers in Williamsburg. They emphasized that the governing body of the state should be made up of average citizens who would meet every two years (now yearly) to draft the laws necessary to the well being of the Commonwealth.

When the state began to govern itself, the legislators were farmers, large plantation owners, small shop owners, and craftsmen. The economy revolved around agriculture so it was easy enough for the elected officials to pack-off to Richmond for a couple of months in January and February. Obviously, and unfortunately, this is not the case today. We no longer live in a society where you can close up your small shop for two months every year. Even small farmers would be hard pressed to take off for two months in the dead of winter today. The time and the cost for the individual lawmaker is prohibitive.

Despite the personal expense and the strain of traveling and being away from my business and family while I served in the General Assembly, as an infamous Republican used to say, "Let me make something perfectly clear." I am not complaining. I am proud and honored to have served the people of my legislative district, and the people of Virginia. I am thankful that I had the personal resources which allowed me the time to serve in Richmond. I also enjoyed the service on many important committees which necessitated extra trips to the state capitol each year. My family and I have greatly benefited from our state and its rich resources, and the privilege of serving in the House of Delegates has outweighed any inconvenience or sacrifice we may have felt.

The first time I ran for state office I was busy operating a small grocery store/gas station, and working extra hours as a carpenter's helper. I had the desire and the ambition to serve; but, realistically speaking, it is a good thing that I didn't win. It would not have been practical for me to leave my business at that time for two months.

I am extremely pleased with the caliber of my peers in the House of Delegates and my colleagues in the Senate, but I feel the intent of the founding fathers would be better served if a more diverse group were sitting in Mr. Jefferson's building in Richmond. It bothers me that the guy who pumps gas does not have much of a chance to be elected to serve in the Virginia Legislature. It concerns me that the woman who bags my groceries has a doubtful opportunity to take her views to the governing body of the state. It's not fair that the man who works long hours building roads over and through the mountains of southwest Virginia has little chance to talk about this vital issue to state delegates and senators. Mothers, telephone operators, accountants, coal miners, production line workers, nurses, and other workers should have the opportunity to campaign, be elected, and to serve in the legislative body that makes the laws and sets the policies by which they live. That would be true participatory democracy!

What about this idea? On selected years legislators go to work in the place of another qualified citizen who has not had a chance to serve because of time or money, but had been approved by the voters. This would not be an ideal situation (there would still be some unable to serve), but it would open up the process to a larger segment of the population. I believe this service is an honor and privilege every responsible citizen should have.

I think the interests of the Commonwealth would be better served if its legislative body were more representative of the general population. At this time, fifty-seven percent of the legislators are attorneys which is nine percent higher than the next state, Texas. The attorney-legislators are highly qualified individuals, but this makes for an unrepresentative body. My criticism of the restrictive nature of who can serve, and the disproportionate socio-economic make-up, is not derived at my design, but are simple facts of life in Virginia. Many of my colleagues share my opinion. I believe it would be of great service to the Commonwealth if the Legislature would devote some time and thought to any factors believed, even if unintentional, to maintain the "citizen legislature" our forefathers envisioned.

CHAPTER 7

DON'S WORDS: I HAD A LIFE-LONG DREAM...

My beginning in politics was something less than auspicious. My first two attempts at elected office were unsuccessful. These were in the Democratic primaries of 1967 and 1969. Prior to 1967 I had been encouraged to run for Sheriff of Tazewell County by two friends who had long been involved in politics, Rhea Moore, Clerk of the Court, and Judge Wade Coates. I had served on the police force in Richmond for a while when I first got out of the Marines, and that prompted them to surmise in 1965 that I had enough experience to handle the job of sheriff. I believe they also thought the Democratic sheriff then serving might not be re-elected.

I was flattered at the suggestions that I run, but I declined since I was operating my own small business and had future plans for my family and for myself. I wanted to expand my financial interests. I wanted my business to grow and I had dreams, many of which have come true, of becoming a successful entrepreneur. Tazewell and southwest Virginia were growing, and I wanted to grow with it. I have always enjoyed new challenges, and for a young man with his own business there was nothing more exciting than growing and developing in business in an area on the brink of change. I feel I did make the right choice because a few years later I owned and rented several houses, had built and owned and operated several apartment projects in Tazewell, as well as the first shopping center locally, and had built the first and only twin-theatre in the area, and was instrumental in establishing the weekly "Free Press."

Don Dunford.

All of the somewhat modest success provided me the opportunity to get involved in politics. This is another reason for rejecting the offer of Moore and Coates. I had a life-long dream of serving in the Virginia

House of Burgesses, as it was originally called, and my relative success gave me a certain independence of time and resources to spend as a legislator. I am pleased with the way things turned out. Probably I would have been more successful in business if I had spent more time in making money and expanding my financial interests. However, I am admittedly restless. I wanted to get into politics to serve the people of southwest Virginia instead of promoting just my own interests. Very fortunately, I have been able to fulfill several dreams and ambitions.

The White House.

Donna and Nancy's mother had never been to the White House. So - I took them. I drove up and drove in. The gatekeeper came immediately and I am sure he noticed my license plate that indicated I was a State Delegate.

I told him "I am here to see my President." I handed him my business card. The gatekeeper looked at me and said, "Just a minute." He came back to my car and said, "Someone will be over." A lady came and escorted us to the White House for a tour.

On our way in, on the front lawn, we ran into Ann Compton, an old friend from WDBJ-TV in Roanoke. She was doing, at that time, the Evening News for ABC-TV from the White House in Washington, D.C. She gave us a hug and we proceeded inside.

To this day, I think the chance meeting with Ann Compton impressed our host to the degree that we were given a complete tour including the Oval Office. The President was out of town for which they apologized.

Two years later Nancy and I were invited to dinner at The White House. We were in Richmond for the waining days of the General Assembly. My Dad was also in Richmond visiting my sisters. As Nancy and I were going out the door the phone rang - The person on the end said "This is the Tazewell Community Hospital, Mr. Dunford your Mother just passed away." As you can imagine, I picked up my Dad and came home immediately. I missed The President again.

CHAPTER 8

DON'S WORDS: OFF TO RICHMOND...

1971 was a significant year for politics in Virginia, especially for the Democrats and double special for me. It was the year Virginia went under the new constitution. Most significant of new changes was the switch in the General Assembly meetings from every two years to annual meetings. I did not interpret this change as a result of the appearance of Don Dunford on the legislative scene.

Another change of importance to me was in my legislative district which now included all of Tazewell, Russell, and Buchanan Counties. Also, as I have mentioned before, it was the year the local Democrats held a convention instead of a primary. I believe I could have won a primary that year. I lost by 111 votes two years before and my name recognition was increasing. The party regulars who were likely to participate in the convention knew and liked me. Among party people I felt I had a better chance of defeating Dalton.

Of statewide importance in 1971 was the Democratic convention in Roanoke to choose a nominee for a special election for the office of lieutenant governor. The 1969 election had seen the election of Virginia's first Republican governor in this century, Linwood Holton. Also elected was the very popular Lt. Governor, J. Sargent Reynolds, a Democrat. 1969 also saw the election of a Democratic Attorney General, Andrew P. Miller, son of a former candidate for governor and the U.S. Senate, Frances Pickens Miller, the anti-Byrd politician of the late forties and early fifties.

Tragedy struck J. Sargent Reynolds, the man many thought would be a future governor, a future senator, and perhaps the first president from the South in modern times. He died of a brain tumor. Virginia voters had a special election in 1971 to fill his unexpired term.

Let me say something here about my races. In 1967 and 1969, I ran a strong campaign based on personality. I did have to talk about issues. My platform included: election for school boards, amendment of the auto titling tax, improved roads which was always a prime issue in southwest Virginia where the majority of roads are secondary, no general tax increase, a four year college for Tazewell County, assurance of the value of a home paid to anyone whose home is taken for any reason by the state or county, new industry and new jobs for the state and particularly in the southwest, flood control, more parks, black lung bill, and curbs on beef imports.

Don Dunford Voting.

I was off to Richmond to represent the people of the Third Legislative District of Virginia. Though I knew enough history and read the papers enough to have a basic working knowledge of how the Legislature operated, there was no way I, or any other freshman delegate, could have enough understanding to jump into the process with arms and legs flailing. It takes time to familiarize yourself with the issues, the procedures, the bureaucratic maze, and the personalities of the men and women in this most important process. It is true that people have a right to expect their representatives to go into the legislative body on an equal footing with the other elected members; but in reality, it takes time to learn a new job. This fact, unfortunately, keeps many politicians in office too long, and keeps many a fine and capable individual out of public service. The seniority system and the knowledge of how to get things done are strong arguments to keep incumbents in office. No one wants to think he is not being adequately represented because the elected official needs on-the-job training.

I do not believe this actually happens to any serious extent in either legislative body. When I first went to the House of Delegates in 1972, I was a member of one of the largest freshmen classes in history. Neither I nor my fellow freshman delegates had a detailed knowledge of many of the issues, but most of us had a working knowledge, especially of the most important issues affecting our constituencies. I had as much, or more, first hand knowledge of the need for secondary roads in southwest Virginia as any delegate, present or past. I knew how my constituents felt about government spending. Often someone new will actually have a better understanding of the mood and wishes of the people than a representative who has been in office for many years and has lost touch with the folks back home.

Not all aspects of representing are equal though. The informational part of being a good delegate may be readily available to the freshman and incumbent alike, but the knowledge and ability to put it to good use takes a little longer to acquire. I believe when I first sat down in the House Chamber I had the ability to vote intelligently on the vast majority of bills what came up during that session.

The area where I, and other newcomers, needed time to prepare ourselves was in introducing new legislation. You need to know where to get pertinent information relating to a bill, and you need to know who is for and against a specific bill. In addition, you need to know how to get other people to support your bills. This is known as orchestrating a bill, and believe me, it's a difficult process. It's all part of the political procedure.

You have to remember that a bill must not only pass in the House where you can argue its merits before fellow delegates, but it must also pass the Senate where your voice will not be heard. Then your bill must be signed by the governor. This is one of the reasons the governor has so much power. At this time there is no provision in the Virginia Constitution for over-riding a veto by the governor. An important piece of legislation could be stopped at any of these junctures, or it could never get out of the appropriate committee in the first place. The legislative process is a slow, long process, but it is meant to be and I agree with the process. However, you can see the extent to which an effective legislator has to go for a bill to pass. A good politician must be a good mechanic.

When I first got to Richmond I chose the wise road and decided to wait and learn the process thoroughly before acting too much on my own. I studied under Don McGlothlin. Our constituents were the same and he had quite a bit more experience. In addition to serving in the House, Don had also served in the Senate, a distinction no one else in the House could claim. His guidance was extremely helpful, and I believe my orientation quickened because of McGlothlin's influence. He advised me to always vote no, when in doubt.

The most important piece of legislation I was involved with in the General Assembly was a proposal I

Don McGlothlin.

Don Dunford.

vehemently opposed. It was the state wide coal severance tax proposed by Republican Governor Mills Godwin in 1976. My fellow delegate, Don McGlothlin, and I fought long and hard against this unfair tax.

The governor asked for a four percent state coal severance tax to go into the general revenue fund. McGlothlin and I had already introduced and gotten the first local severance tax, one half of one percent. We were not opposed to the local tax, and neither were the coal operators or the miners themselves. The local tax was a great boon to the people of the coal producing counties of southwest Virginia. With the increased emphasis on the use of "King Coal" in the past few years, the economy of a poor section of Virginia had been growing at an incredible rate. Everyone in the southwest counties had benefited greatly.

The local severance tax has allowed southwest Virginians to improve their roads and schools, two vital concerns. The tax is small to the operators who pay it, and they can see the direct affects on the lives of the people around them. The coal operators understand poverty, and they have experienced the step-child attitude from the Richmond lawmakers toward the local needs. The people of southwest Virginia generally feel their needs must be met through local government with as little interference as possible from the state and national levels. For years the powers-that-be in Richmond failed in the responsibility for the well being of this one section of the state. When we finally began solving our own problems, the Republican administration felt our solution could solve some of their spending problems, too. I, for one, was not going to stand by and watch the executive branch of the state government treat the people of my district in the same manner they had come to expect for many years.

This issue in 1976 had an even greater significance to the over-all political scene in Virginia. This was the first time in memory that someone took on the governor of the state and won.

Governor Mills Godwin had many friends in the General Assembly, on both sides of the political fence, and he was confident that he would get his state severance tax. The governor of Virginia is the most powerful executive in the nation, according to some political analysts. He makes more direct appointments than the president of the United States. He is powerful, and I did not intend to "take on" such a figure on any issue. However, the coal severance tax was a life blood issue, in my opinion, for my constituents. Neither Don McGlothin nor I could have been elected again, or should have been, if we had failed to stand up for the rights of voters on this issue.

In an impassioned speech before the finance committee of the House of Delegates, I implored my fellow delegates to defeat the proposal with these words: "This proposition is a means by which the Commonwealth of Virginia can rape the coal producing counties of Virginia…without (the local severance tax), in some instances, it is conceivable that local property taxes would increase ten-fold."

After the speech, I am told, Eleanor Sheppard, one of my colleagues, declared, "Patrick Henry lives on."

I thank her for the compliment, intentional or not.

The coal severance tax issue was one of the most important questions I had to deal with. The well being of the people of my district, and my function as their representative, were at stake, and I intended to leave no possible tactic untried to stop this legislation. If I had lost the battle, I was going to be able to tell my constituents that, at least, I had fired all my guns, There is never any point after debate to sit at home and say to yourself, "I should have said…"

Don Dunford watches the House Finance kill the Coal Tax.

Don Dunford & Don McGlothlin.

Don Dunford & Don McGlothlin.

Don Dunford's Grandparents on their wedding day in November of 1902.

Amelia Bell Harman

Born - October 12, 1886
Died - November 30, 1984

Tom D. Dunford

Born - 1883
Died - June 5, 1969

CHAPTER 9

PEOPLE WHO MAKE THINGS HAPPEN: SENATOR GEORGE F. BARNES...

Senator George F. Barnes.

Senator George Barnes was a decent man in every respect. He grew up decent and remained decent throughout his political service. He was a great Virginian and a great Tazewell Countian. He served his constituents well as a member of the Senate of Virginia.

During the time we served together, George in the Senate and me in the House of Delegates, we rode to and from Richmond together many times. During those trips we discussed everything from politics to religion. Perhaps of most importance were our discussions of issues that would benefit Tazewell and Virginia citizens.

George Barnes and I agreed politically and philosophically 98% of the time. We both had a southern conservative democratic philosophy of government. There was never any animosity because we were on opposite sides of the political fence. We realized a mutual respect has to exist between rivals in political parties since their goals are the same: to represent all of the people to the best of our ability.

I remember the specific occasion when the people of Tazewell, led by the Rev. W.F. Wadsworth, had a plan for a park in the town. The plans and ideas needed federal funds to become a reality. George Barnes and I took the town's request, with the plans and maps and ideas, and drove to

Washington to present them to our United States congressmen and senators. We had lunch in the Senate Dining Room with our senators. Consequently the grant came through and the Tazewell Recreation Park was built.

Lincolnshire Park - Lake.

That's only one example of our doing things together. It would have been stupid for us to travel to Washington separately since we had the same goal in mind. We respected each other politically and personally, and I think Tazewell County, and the state, were better off because of it.

George Barnes is one of those Tazewell County people who put his heart and his efforts in promoting what he thought was right and good.

CHAPTER 10

PEOPLE WHO MAKE THINGS HAPPEN: ON THE CAMPAIGN TRAIL...

To campaign in Tazewell means travel from community to community, often stopping at country stores. This was the way old time politicians had done it. In the campaign days of Wade Coates and Rhea Moore (Commonwealth's Attorney and Clerk of the Court) an individual would go to Tannersville and stop at Penland's Store, and then Holmes Grocery, to leave campaign literature. Rural stores were the heartbeat of politics in these communities, from Joe Harris' Store in 'Possum Hollow to Mustard's Store a couple of miles away in Thompson Valley. George Mustard was commissioner of the revenue, a Democrat, and Joe Harris was a leader in the Republican Party in the fifties.

When Chuck Robb was campaigning for lieutenant governor in 1977, his campaign staff sent him to Tazewell County to spend a day and night with me. At that time the most pressing problem in Tazewell County was the deplorable condition of our secondary roads. I was always trying to get road funds. I believed Chuck Robb would be elected, and would be an influential figure in Virginia government in the coming years. I thought it was important for him to ride over every mile of secondary roads in the county, to stop at all the country stores, to distribute as much campaign literature as possible in order to solicit votes.

Chuck and I traveled from Tazewell to Richlands to Raven to Jewell Ridge, on to Bandy and Baptist Valley and Amonate and Abbs Valley. Then we went to Boissevain, Pocahontas, Bluefield, Clear Fork, Thompson Valley, over many miles of secondary roads. We started in the early morning and didn't get back to my house until

Don Dunford with Chuck Robb.

midnight. Both of us were tired. Nancy greeted us at the door and asked Chuck if there was anything he would like to eat or drink before going to bed.

"Don, do you normally eat before retiring?" asked Chuck.

"I eat a big bait every night before I go to bed."

"What is a bait?" asked Chuck.

"It's about a five course meal."

Chuck laughed and said he would like to have a glass of milk and some cookies.

That happened in 1977 and I forgot about the milk and cookies incident until January of 1990 in Richmond when we were at a gala in honor of Governor Wilder, Lt. Governor Beyer, and Attorney General Mary Sue Terry. Willard Scott was there and he told the story of staying at the governor's mansion, compliments of Chuck Robb, some five years earlier. As the evening progressed, he and Chuck went upstairs to the private quarters and had milk and tollhouse cookies.

Chuck has not changed much. He is still a milk and cookie man, and more power to him.

Don, Nancy, & Don Beyer.

Don, Nancy, & Mary Sue Terry.

CHAPTER 11

PEOPLE WHO MAKE THINGS HAPPEN: GOVERNORS OF VIRGINIA...

I was a Democrat in the House of Delegates for eight years. My entire eight years were spent serving with Republican governors. I started out in 1972 with Governor Linwood Holton, then with Governor John Dalton, and Governor Mills Godwin.

All three are remembered as great Virginians. They served within the confines of fiscal responsibility, integrity, and good old southern democratic principles. I recall each of them with a certain amount of affection and fondness.

One evening I saw Governor Holton at a cocktail party. He put his arm around me and said, "Dunford, I like you."

I looked at him and said, "Governor, how in the world could you like me? I voted against your bonds today."

The governor looked me in the eye and said, "I always know where you stand."

That was a lesson to me. Always let people know where you stand, regardless of the side you are on and they will respect you.

I had the privilege of sitting on House committees with Governor John Dalton because he was in the House of Delegates before becoming lieutenant governor and governor. John was such a decent man that he would give you the proverbial "coat off of his back." When supporting legislation he judged all sides on their merits and did not play partisan politics.

There had been discussion for years about a veterinary school at Virginia Tech. One day I took it upon myself to go to legislative services and have a bill drawn which would create a veterinary school. With the bill in my pocket I solicited patrons and within two or three days I had 71 patrons. It could have been a totally political issue. Dick Bagley was chairman of the Appropriations Committee, controlled by Democrats. However, Governor Dalton made no bones about his interest in the proposed veterinary school, and he permitted my bill to be written into the budget. It subsequently became a reality. That was the kind of man John Dalton was. Although, before I introduced the bill, the Governor and Bill Lavery both tried to get me to wait until next year. If I had waited, the Veterinary School may not have been, because of next years budget.

Vet School Bill Cost: $2.5 Million

By OZZIE OSBORNE
Richmond Bureau

RICHMOND — Delegate Don Dunford, D-Tazewell, has introduced legislation that would establish a school of veterinary medicine at Virginia Tech that is signed by 78 House members, in addition to Dunford.

That apparently assures it of approval by the 100 member House.

The bill calls for an appropriation of $2.5 million in the next budget period.

Of this amount, $1.2 million would be used for operations and $1.3 million would be used for interim housing for the school.

Signed Virginia Tech Veterniary School Bill.

Perhaps Mills Godwin's greatest contribution to the Commonwealth was the sales tax. How can that be? We look at the sales tax proposed by Governor Godwin and it reminds us of the transportation tax proposed by Governor Baliles. Without the sales tax Virginia would not have the community college system. Governor Godwin had to call for taxation to finance such a tremendous undertaking as the college system.

Governor Baliles came out of his corner swinging when he was in the state's highest office. He ran the state with an iron hand and set Virginia on its course for the 21st century. He came out of a conservative mold, but he was a moderate governor. The

Don Dunford with Governor Baliles.

contribution he made to transportation for the 21st century includes the gas tax, used for building new roads. This tax, studied in one way, becomes an actual savings to the taxpayers. Imagine a highway between points X and Y. Travel over that highway now takes two hours and $5 worth of gas. You raise the gas tax by 5% and with the increase you build a road. When you build the road the travel time is cut by one hour. Time, of course, is money.

By operating your car half the time over a better road the bill is cut to $2.50 although the gas tax has gone up 5%. Then you use the $2.50 worth of gas times 5% so you increase it 12-1/2 cents, so it costs you $2.62-1/2 to ride between the same two points instead of $5.00. This is plus the fact you save an hour, and the new road is safer than the old one. So I submit with this analogy that a gas tax can be a real savings to the people of Virginia.

Governor Baliles did not use that analogy, nor did he seek my advice. Of course, it turned out he didn't need my advice and things worked out well as they were.

On Saturday before Doug Wilder was elected governor on Tuesday, he spent the night at my home. Sunday morning there was a breakfast for the governor, lieutenant governor, attorney general, and the traveling press entourage, at my home. The breakfast didn't start until ten o'clock so Doug

Governor Doug Wilder.

Wilder sat in my kitchen in the early morning drinking coffee and reminiscing about our years in the General Assembly. It was one of the most memorable times of my life. I knew then Doug was destined for great things. He would never again have the time or opportunity to sit at my table, read the paper, and make small talk. I vividly recall Doug's humbleness and his vision for a new Virginia.

Earlier in the year I had picked Doug up in Giles County and he toured Tazewell County on a whirlwind visit. He had an appointment with the editorial staff of the Bluefield Daily Telegraph. Tom Colley, Editor, later told me Doug Wilder was one of the most impressive politicians he had ever interviewed.

Don Dunford & Governor Warner.

Don, Donna, Governor Kaine, Nancy.

CHAPTER 12

PEOPLE WHO MAKE THINGS HAPPEN: PRISON FOR SOUTHWEST VIRGINIA...

Vivian Watts, Governor Baliles Secretary of Transportation and Public Safety, was in total control of the destiny of new prisons in Virginia. Many of us wanted a new prison in southwest Virginia, and the 500 new jobs that would come with it. However, we soon found out Vivian Watts was adamantly opposed to a southwest Virginia facility. I remember talking to Vivian when she told me 70% of individuals incarcerated in Virginia were from the Washington-Richmond-Norfolk corridor. The prisons, she believed, were needed in that area.

I told Vivian we weren't in the 70%, but we were interested in the remaining 30% who could be sent to a prison in the southwest area. Vivian remained cool to the suggestion. I did not give up on the idea, nor did others who knew a prison would give our economy a shot in the arm. At the time I served on the speaker's committee of the Chamber of Commerce, with Joe West, a local banker. We issued an invitation to Vivian to speak at the annual Chamber dinner. Of course, out ulterior motive was to talk to her about the proposed prison.

Vivian accepted the invitation to speak at the dinner, to meet people at a reception, and to spend the night at my home. She accepted on one condition, that she could bring her husband and that I would arrange for him to go trout fishing in what she had heard was the best fishing spot in southwest Virginia. I immediately called Eli Jones, a member of the Virginia Game Commission, who agreed to handle the fishing trip. It was planned that Vivian's husband would set out for the expedition at 4 a.m., so they came to Tazewell very happy people.

Don McGlothlin was delighted when he heard of the Vivian Watts visit. Some of his friends donated a helicopter when he landed at Lincolnshire Park on Sunday afternoon for Vivian and me to board for a flight over potential prison sites in Tazewell and Buchanan Counties. That was well and good and Vivian was pretty well locked in!

The strange thing was that two weeks prior to these plans Nancy and I were driving home from out of state and when we got into Tazewell County Nancy said, "Don, I have always had a dream to see Tazewell County from a helicopter."

"Maybe someday that will be possible," I replied.

When Don McGlothlin set the helicopter ride up for Vivian, I put Nancy on in my place to tour Tazewell and Buchanan County sites from the air.

As the story goes, Don McGlothlin, at 2000 feet, turned to Vivian Watts and said, "We get the prison site here or you go out the door."

"I commit to you. You have the prison," Vivian said.

Whether that happened or not, I don't know. None of them, Vivian, Don, or Nancy will confirm or deny it; but, we do have the prison located in Buchanan County, a great economic boon, and we'll always be grateful to the Baliles administration for it.

CHAPTER 13

PEOPLE WHO MAKE THINGS HAPPEN: A TAZEWELL MUSEUM...

During the mid-seventies when I was in the House, one day I was on the fifth floor of the Capitol preparing for a committee meeting when someone tapped me on the shoulder. It was Nellé White Bundy from Tazewell.

"I need to talk to you. Do you have a minute?" asked Nellé.

"Yes, Nellé," I said. "What do you need?"

"Don, you know some of us in Tazewell County have come up with the idea of a museum. We've done a lot of thinking and planning, but we have no money. If we would get a little seed money we would have a museum, and we came to talk with you here. What do we do?" asked Nellé.

"You just did it. You told me and now consider it done," I said.

I wrote a little amendment to the budget bill and went to my dear friend, Ed Lane, Chairman of the Appropriations Committee at that time. I told Ed that out in Tazewell County we did not ask for much, but we would like to have a little seed money for a museum. Ed, graciously, as chairman, included it in the budget bill.

So, we got funding for the Historic Crab Orchard Museum, which has been of great value to the area and a source of pride.

 *The hospital was dedicated in two days of ceremonies with then-congressman William Wampler as the Keynote Speaker. Wampler, Board Chairman, Sam Ward Bishop, and Nannie Rose Moss Peery cut the ribbon for the facility. Shown in the picture (to the right) are left to right: Sam Ward Bishop, Board Chairman; Carl Gillespie, Jr., Vice Chairman; Mrs. Nannie Rose Peery, and Congressman Wampler. In the background, Don Dunford, Dr. Mary E. Johnston, Dr. Rufus Brittain, Dr. Eduardo Plagata, Senator George Barnes, Mayor Earl Wallace, and the hospital's first administrator, Stanley Omwake.*

CHAPTER 14

PEOPLE WHO MAKE THINGS HAPPEN: THE LADY FROM PATRICK...

Mary Sue Terry.

Mary Sue Terry was elected to the House of Delegates in the midst of my term, so I have known her since her first days as a legislator. She is impressive, smart, and well liked. I was privileged to meet her parents. They are what you would envision "Mr. and Mrs. Virginia" to be.

Mary Sue did her homework, worked hard, and was elected Attorney General, the first woman to be elected to statewide office. She was highly qualified and the electorate of Virginia realized that. Virginia voters, highly intelligent themselves, required their leaders to have dedication and ability.

During her first term as Attorney General, Mary Sue did an outstanding job. She came to Tazewell County on one occasion to speak at the annual Chamber of Commerce dinner. She spent the night at our home and she impressed all who met her.

Mary Sue Terry.

I'm convinced she will be the next governor of the Commonwealth. At the same time the Democrats can be proud that a young man has appeared on the Virginia scene, Don Beyer. He promises to become one of Virginia's finest leaders.

What I'm really saying is that the future of Virginia is in good hands, and the coming years look bright for the Commonwealth.

Robert Galembeck, Don Beyer, Don Dunford.

CHAPTER 15

DON'S STORY: MEMORABLE MOMENTS...

During Don's tenure as a delegate, he made it a point to reach out to the youth of Tazewell County. When he returned from the many trips to Richmond, he would teach a government class to the youth of Tazewell County Public Schools whenever the opportunity arose. He would explain his reason for being in Richmond and what was accomplished during the most recent session.

The energy crisis of 1972 was of the utmost importance to the nation, as well as Virginia with special problems we have to face. The commission was empanelled to study the situation in Virginia and to report to the governor and the General Assembly. Our legislation created a Coal and Energy Center

Destination: Oil Rig in the Gulf.

Don Dunford & George Barnes Stepping onto the Oil Rig.

Don Dunford getting ready for helicopter ride in Gulf of Mexico.

at Virginia Tech as means to help solve the energy problem for future generations. The study commission sent us out to see an oil rig in the Gulf of Mexico. If they were off the coast of Virginia, we would know what they would be like

Don Dunford is an avid Virginia Tech fan was proven by his desire and need to attend every football and basketball game that he can fit into his schedule.

Don Dunford & Frank Beamer.

His appearance at many football games, as well as being former member of the Board of Visitors, has endeared Don to the coaching staff of the football team. When Don had his heart by-pass surgery, he was presented with a gigantic card signed by the coaching staff.

Don was the driving force behind the creation of the Veterinary School at Virginia Tech as well as the Coal and Energy Center.

A little known fact about Don is that he once was a part owner of the WTZE radio station in Tazewell

Don Dunford was part owners of this radio station.

Don Dunford introduced the first bill in the General Assembly, upon the suggestion of Ruth Tarter, to set a specific age and date for children to begin school. This was necessary because many parents would send children that were too young, not yet potty-trained or talking; or, those who would start the first grade at the ages of nine or ten, maybe even older, which was long past first grade age.

In the 70's, the Tazewell Chamber of Commerce found it necessary to search for a new home other than the Coal Building that they were occupying.

Don Dunford explains the School Bill.

During the search Don recalled his visit to Boone, North Carolina, where he noticed that the Chamber of Commerce located in that city had built its own structure, thus not relying on the unstable possibility of renting or leasing space.

Don offered to give them real estate in the 4-Way Shopping Plaza but another offer came from the owner of the mall where Magic Mart is currently located. The chamber members did not take his offer of land but they used the separate structure idea of Don's to build their own Tazewell County Chamber of Commerce Building. Earl Levois ran with the idea.

When Don was elected to the Board of Supervisors, Tazewell County was three million dollars in the red. Needless to say, Don was one of the key players who put the county in the black – without raising taxes.

Don Dunford was instrumental in saving the county twenty million dollars for the construction of a new school to replace Graham High School that was suffering from a sinkhole problem. Rather than construct a new high school, the more cost effective decision of filling the holes and making the necessary repairs was pursued.

We have our Tazewell County Fair every August because Don urged his fellow supervisors to start it up again. I, for one, am so glad he did that. I love the fair and look forward to its arrival every year where I work as a volunteer.

In order to help the fair along on its way to being the best it could be, Don was responsible for appropriating county money for the construction of Nuckolls Hall.

Don donated several acres of land located across from Tazewell Middle School for industrial development. In addition, Don gave several acres of land to the Town of Tazewell for the creation of the Don Dunford Park which provides more playground area for Tazewell youth.

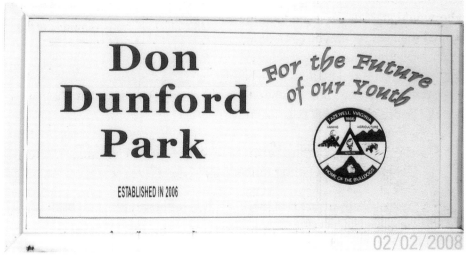

Don Dunford Park.

Don donated building lots and cash to the creation of the Tazewell Wellness Center, now the YMCA.

During his term on the Public Service Authority of
Tazewell County,
Don has had a hand in these completed projects:
     Bishop & Amonate Water Systems
     Bluefield to Springville Water
     Raven/Doran Water System Upgrade
     Pounding Mill Quarry Water Line Extension
     Jewell Ridge Water-Phase II
     Johnson Hollow Water Project
     Smith Ridge Community Water (Self Help) (First in
     Virginia)
     Peel Chestnut (Self Help)
The following projects were under construction when Don
Dunford completed his term on the PSA:
     Baptist Valley Water
     Springville to Divides
     Claypool Hill to Pounding Mill
     Wardell
     Falls Mills (Self Help)
     Red Root Ridge
     Drytown
     St. Clair's Crossing
The sewer projects that were
completed are:
     Bluefield to Divides
     Tazewell to Divides
     Gratton
     Baptist Valley – Phase I
     Amonate
     Tazewell to Pounding Mill
     Claypool Hill to Pounding Mill

*East River Tunnel Groundbreaking -
Supervisor Graham Hendrick, Judge
Vince Sexton, High Engineer Howard
Shepherd, Delegate Don Dunford.*

As the result of the Senate of Virginia appointing Don Dunford to a
"Study of the Safe Drinking Water Needs in Southwest Virginia", the needs
were identified. Tazewell County was successful in getting sixteen million
of thirty-two million dollars Washington allotted to the entire state.

A scholarship for a Tazewell High School student to attend Southwest
Virginia Community College has been endowed by Don & Nancy Dunford.
Again, he is striving to help the youth of Tazewell County.

The East River Tunnel is of one of the wonders of this region and
Don Dunford was there for the turning of the first shovel of dirt.

My darling daughter Donna.

Of all the memorable moments he has included in this chapter, his most important one would be the birth of his daughter, Donna.

Donna.

Donna & her Harp - Donna studied at the Peabody School at John Hopkins University. She has played for Governor Wilder at the Governor's Mansion as well as a Reception at the Virginia Museum.

Don & Nancy relaxing.

Don gets the pleasure of traveling to the beach several times a year. He and Nancy truly love walking in the sand.

Don & Nancy having fun.

CHAPTER 16

DON'S STORY: DEAR FRIENDS….

Many of Don's friends are politicians but many of his friends are not. This is a smattering of both worlds:

Friend George Dickenson.

Don's Friends Reminisce...

DON'S STORY – PEGGY AND PHILIP AVERETT

In late summer of 1983 while reading a book on the shore of beautiful Cheery Grove Beach, South Carolina, a man spoke casually as he walked by. This was not unusual, as vacationers are always relaxed and friendly. A few minutes later friends from Delaware, who were staying with us, came down to the beach and we formed a semi-circle and started

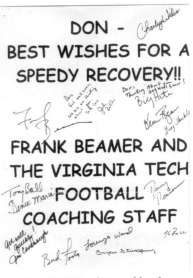

Get Well Card signed by the Virginia Tech Football Coaching Staff.

Averetts & Dunfords at Mountain Lake.

talking and catching up with one another. The man who had spoken to me earlier came back by as we were talking about Concord College where he overheard us and introduced himself saying he, too, had attended Concord. Thus, being neighbors in a beach cottage located across from each other, a wonderful friendship was formed.

There are people God puts in our lives for many reasons and Don and his wife, Nancy, are very special to us. They have become a huge part of our family. We can't imagine our lives without them. We have been together during happy occasions like weddings of our children and then the births of our grandchildren. They were there during sad times as well, with the death of my sister. They were always there, helping and being very supportive in every way.

Of course, you can't know Don and not be introduced to "The Hokies." We have tailgated and gone to many games. There were games in the rain, snow, storms with lightning, and beautiful sunny days. There is nothing like the excitement of the game!!!

Over the years we have visited in Tazewell and have witnessed Don and Nancy's generosity and love for others. If they knew a person in need they were always eager to provide help. Their lovely home has always been open to people whether it be two or two hundred. They are the perfect host and hostess.

We love Don and Nancy and have been blessed by their friendship.

DON'S STORY: BILL TUCK

Bill Tuck - 1961.

Bill Tuck, owner of TuckIt In Storage in Blacksburg, Virginia, tells me that he and Don Dunford have been friends for nearly fifty years. They were both on the Concord College football team as well as fraternity brothers and they never allowed that friendship to end. Mr. Tuck pointed out that their friendship is not one that is reinforced by the sight of each other daily. They will go for about four or five years with no contact and then run into each other at a chance meeting and it was just like the good old college days except that they both are a little grayer.

At one of those chance meetings at the Red Lion in Blacksburg, Bill heard a familiar voice. He knew he had to peek around the corner to find out if it really was his old friend, Don Dunford, who was doing all of talking and laughing.

While catching up on events of the past years, Bill mentioned that he had started up The Montgomery County Free Press.

A seed was planted in Don's brain that started to take root bringing forth the Tazewell County Free Press that covered the news from Bluefield to Richlands and all of the surrounding county areas.

Bill helped Don get his newspaper business started by telling him what he would need and recommending printers and coping with anything that might crop up in Don's path to becoming a newspaperman.

Bill tells the tale of the get together of friends to go 'coon hunting with no killing of any kind of animal involved. All of the men, with the exception of Don, showed up in the hunting attire you would expect. Don was wearing really nice clothes not designed for 'coon hunting but he wanted to go no matter how he was dressed. Even though Don calls himself just a country boy, he never appeared to be that country boy.

Bill says that Don was always a leader and very active in their college years.

"Don is a person of influence and when you become a friend of Don's, you are always a friend. Time does not diminish the relationship."

He remembers that Don was never afraid to get involved in something he believed in and that includes friendship.

Bill describes Don as a good person and an upfront character who tells you how it's going to be with whatever endeavor he plans to tackle.

Above all else, Bill Tuck describes Don Dunford as the ultimate: HOKIE FAN.

DON'S STORY:
DR. CHARLES R. KING

Dr. Charles R. King, Past President of the Southwest Virginia Community College, allowed me to ask him some questions about his relationship with Don Dunford on November 19, 2009.

It was 1973 late in the day just before adjournment of the General Assembly.

I was outside working in the yard decked out in my coveralls and raggedy shirt when the telephone rang.

Dr. Charles R. King.

"Can you use a building?" ask the familiar voice at the other end of the telephone conversation.

"Yes, I can," I responded without any thought at all.

"How big?"

"40,000 square feet."

"I'm horse-trading here, Charlie. I'll get back to you," and then the line was dead. I stood there for a moment pondering the conversation but not really giving it much credence.

We talked back and forth two or three times.

A couple of hours later, I was still working in the yard when the telephone rang again.

"You got it. You got your building, Charlie," said Don Dunford as his smile could be felt through the telephone lines.

It was the last day of the General Assembly session and it went down to the wire.

That was how Tazewell Hall came into being.

Don deserved a lot of the credit. If he hadn't been there at just the right time, we wouldn't have gotten the building. We didn't deserve it. We weren't qualified for it. But – we got it.

I was tickled with Don and ever so grateful.

We should have had to wait another 10 years, but fortunately we didn't have to do so.

DON'S STORY – SENATOR PHILLIP P. PUCKETT

I spoke with David T. Larimer II, Legislative Assistant, in lieu of speaking directly to Senator Phillip P. Puckett about dealings he may have had with Don Dunford. Mr. Larimer told me the story of the bridges.

Don Dunford called Senator Puckett and asked that a bridge be named after former Senator George F. Barnes in recognition of all the fine work he had performed for the people of southwest Virginia.

"I'm going to do one better than that," replied Senator Puckett. "I'll get a bridge named after both of them, George Barnes and Don Dunford. They should both be recognized."

David continues with the story saying that the Senator was unable to get his task accomplished because, at that point in time, a decision had been made to name bridges for notable persons after they were deceased. Obviously, that meant George Barnes and Don Dunford were still with us on this Earth.

Senator Phillip P. Puckett.

The bridge before exit three off of Route 460 to Tazewell eventually became the "George F. Barnes" bridge and maybe, at some future date, the bridge before one of the other four exits will be named for C. Donald Dunford.

As to why the Town of Tazewell received so many exits and entrances on and off of Route 460? That can be explained by the mention of three names: Don McGlothlin, George Barnes, and Don Dunford.

According to David Larimer all three of the gentlemen worked hard at getting the by-pass around Tazewell with the multitude of exits.

Senator Puckett was gracious enough to call me and confirm the story as related to me by David Larimer. It was indeed an honor to talk with the Senator.

DON'S STORY – DOYLE RASNICK

Senator Reasor, Norman Cook, Doyle Rasnick & Friends at Reception.

My old friend Don Dunford is responsible for my being here in Tazewell County.

My wife, Linda, and I were both employed at Mountain Empire Community College in Big Stone Gap with good jobs that most likely would have lasted until we were ready for retirement.

I received a phone call from Don Dunford telling me that he was interested in starting a newspaper in Tazewell County and he needed a printing business to accompany it.

After talking it over with Linda, we decided we should jump at the chance. We pulled up stakes from Gate City and relocated to Tazewell County Virginia with the birth of Clinch Valley Printing.

Don got his printer for his newly created Tazewell County Free Press. Linda and I started on our exciting path of being owners of a business in the world of printing.

News Years Day 1977 was the birth of Clinch Valley Printing Company, in a 30 x 60 area at the 4-Way Shopping Plaza between Dr. Ben Susman's Office and the Dairy Queen.

Four of us pooled resources of $1,250 each and Clinch Valley Printing was under way. Don was only 25% owner in our printing business but he stayed and worked alongside of me when we had a pressing printing job to complete. I owned 25% at the beginning of the business and the remaining 50% was investors. Clinch Valley Printing evolved from there and so did my friendship with Don Dunford.

Don was already an established businessman and politician so he was more than willing to give me his advice on the do's and don'ts of the business world. As a matter of fact, he gave me his input on running the business whether I wanted it or not. I learned more about what not to do from him than I actually learned about what I should do. Sometimes the hours were long and unrelenting but Don was right there. He was extremely helpful. Today the printing business is technology driven and is no longer based on Ben Franklin's methods of by-gone days.

I feel lucky and blessed to have made Tazewell my home. What a great place to raise my family. Without Don's help, I would never have known Fred Combs and Bill Deskins, two of the men I admired most in my life. Clinch Valley Printing has afforded my family and me the opportunity to travel the world. The security of the community college system would not have permitted that. Today, I own one hundred percent of the company. Although Don is no longer my business partner, we have remained friends over the years.

Don always thought "big" and we were lucky to have him to help us get started. He always wanted things done right and was very difficult to please. Maybe that's why I have succeeded. I had to do it right. Thanks Don.

As of August 2012 Doyle and Linda Rasnick have officially retired from Clinch Valley Printing. The company was sold to Richard and Susan Weaver who still run it to this day at the same location in Tazewell Virginia.

DON'S STORY – DAVID WHITE

David White.

David White was a student at Emory & Henry College just finishing his junior year and seeking a job. He talked to the Assistant Football Coach, Bill Peery, and was told he should check with Don Dunford in Tazewell.

During previous summers David had worked in the Washington, D.C. area for good money, but the living costs were commensurate with the larger take home pay.

Don offered David a job at the Mohawk Tire Store that consisted of changing and selling tires among other duties.

He returned to Don's employ after he obtained his economics degree in his senior year working from May until August. He left in August to begin a job coaching and teaching in Christiansburg. He toiled at the coaching/teaching job for a year and decided it wasn't for him.

David returned to Tazewell and worked for Don again.

He recalls fondly that after his first summer working for Don, that Don bought him his first car – a Dodge Valiant.

Don told David that he used to think someone had to be smart to make a lot of money, but he no longer thinks that. Now, he believes you just got to have the balls to get out and take a chance.

He goes on with the baseball analogy that you can't steal a base with both feet planted firmly on first.

Don was trying to plant the idea in David's mind that he should go into business for himself.

David explains that he wanted to do just that so he moved to Roanoke and started his own tire company to seek his fortune.

Don had suggested that he might go into a partnership with him but David said no. He didn't want to take a chance on losing someone else's money. Besides the fact that he wanted to see if he could do it on his own.

Don tried to talk him into coming back to Tazewell and starting his business but David decided against that. He did get a lot of pointers from Don.

David spent six or seven years growing his business in Roanoke and got into the commercial aspect working with companies and truck fleets. David expanded his tire company in Roanoke to cover the Mid-Atlantic States with fifty million dollars in sales. He sold out to Bridgestone Tire Company and retired to Florida where he is now living.

Eventually he bought Don's tire company but that didn't work out too well because he was an absentee owner.

While David was working with Don he would go house to house campaigning for him during his delegate years.

David got to know Don well over the years and feels that Don Dunford was a positive influence.

He laughs when he thinks about Don's Richmond cohorts. They would have been so surprised if they had come to Tazewell to see Don's flourishing tire business. David described it as a dinky, little store that cost about $2,500 to build and was located at the Four Way Shopping Plaza.

DON'S STORY – DONNA MURRAY

The man I know as Don Dunford is one who will give his total support to anyone that is trying to establish a business or career in this community. He is everyone's best cheerleader.

He wants to succeed in life, but he also wants you to succeed.

In 1984, I wanted to start a nursing practice of my own, so I began to look for a business location. I went everywhere in the area, at least, four times, but the only building I could find that would meet my needs was in the Four Way Shopping Plaza. Don Dunford was the owner of that shopping plaza.

I had nothing to lose and everything to gain so I called his office for an appointment to discuss the possibility of leasing or renting the space from him.

It wasn't exactly what I needed when I finally got a chance to walk through the space, but Don and I talked about it in depth. We negotiated and made sure I could afford to make the monthly payments. He told me I could reconfigure the office to fit my needs.

My personal experience with Don Dunford started with that first practice. He was always there for advice and I appreciated all the help I could get.

When I ran into financial difficulties, he worked with me anyway he could to keep the practice going and to help the business establish a footing in the community.

When my business partnership broke up, he helped me find office furniture to replace the items that were removed by my former partner.

Don liked the idea that my business was a service to take care of the people of the community.

Other memories include the time when I was taking a watercolor class and the Dunford's allowed the entire class to spend the day in his garden painting pictures. They were so gracious and generous as well as patient with us as we trampled through their private world.

The elderly of the area are grateful for the rentals of living space that he has built for their use. He looks after his people because he really cares.

I remember a Halloween Party that my husband Jack and I hosted that Don and Nancy attended. When he showed up he was not wearing a costume or mask. When asked why? He replied, "Don't laugh. This is my Halloween mask."

What I like best about Don is that it doesn't matter who you are, if he can help in anyway, he will. Once he becomes your friend, he is your friend for life. He never changes.

DON'S STORY – J.C. STEELE

J.C. Steele says that he and Don Dunford have been friends since they attended elementary school.

J.C. reminisces about the third grade and a teacher by the name of Ella Bryant Dickenson who was very dedicated to her students.

Ms. Dickenson taught the arts to Tazewell Elementary

Don Dunford and J.C. Steele.

students. She decided it would be good to start a rhythm group with her students exposing them to a different form of music. The instruments would consist of one drum, several triangles, and blocks of wood covered with sandpaper that the player would rub together creating a brushing sound.

When the playing started, there was no music, only rhythm. In order to maintain the cacophony of sounds they would follow the pattern of hit on 1, rest on 2, hit on 3, rest on 4, and continue until the composition was concluded.

The little band was known as the "Tazewell Rhythm Makers."

Ms. Dickenson also taught singing and dancing to the girls and the boys. J.C. and Don were recognized as good dancers by all who watched.

In one of her little performance programs, a little ditty was sung called "The Powhatan Arrow" that was set to the music of "She'll Be Comin' 'Round the Mountain".

The Powhatan Arrow was a Norfolk & Western passenger train that ran from Norfolk, Virginia, to Cincinnati, Ohio, during the 1940's and '50's.

When the song was performed by J.C. Steele and Don Dunford, they were accompanied on the piano by none other than Louise Leslie.

Ms. Dickenson put together a little play for her students to perform for family entertainment.

Don Dunford was Captain John Smith

J.C. Steele was Chief Powhatan.

Nellie Waddell, a fellow classmate, was Pocahontas.

The play had a really memorable scene that was so fantastically performed by the young students that they were asked to present the play to the high school students.

The scene was where Captain John Smith expressed his love interest in Pocahontas. Chief Powhatan became so upset about the idea that he captured John Smith and placed his head on the chopping block. Chief Powhatan would execute John Smith thereby eliminating the problem.

Things didn't go as planned by Chief Powhatan because Pocahontas intervened pleading for the life of Captain John Smith thus sparing his life.

J.C. states that to this day members of the Virginia Republican Party have never forgiven him (Chief Powhatan) for allowing Don Dunford (Captain John Smith) to live.

After the school years, J.C. and Don went different directions but neither wound up on Broadway or in Hollywood; however, they remain special friends to this day.

DON'S STORY – JIM RAMEY

"Don and I played football in high school together," says Jim Ramey, prominent businessman in Tazewell County and surrounding areas. "Don was an outstanding football player and we played together on Tazewell High Schools only undefeated football team during the 1951 season. Don was a good all around student and made all-state as a member of the high school choir.

We ran around together in our youth and actually double-dated at times.

"Don knew what he wanted and he worked hard to accomplish his goal. He had tunnel vision and went after everything he did. He put on his blinders and worked and worked until he succeeded.

"He has always been well disciplined and lives his life accordingly. He is doing well financially after his modest investments and re-investments.

"I believe he has given away more than he has

Jim Ramey

made but that is Don Dunford. He is not a world traveler. He has always been a nice, honest person and someone I am proud to know.

"Years ago, Don and I were flying from Bristol to Atlanta. Once up in air. Don called the stewardess over to ask if we were over the Smoky Mountains because he could see snowy mountaintops. She replied, "Those are not mountains, those are just clouds.""

DON'S STORY – JIM SPENCER

Jim Spencer.

It was a privilege to be the PSA (Public Service Authority) Administrator while Mr. Dunford served on the Board of Directors. He was a man with a vision for moving Tazewell County forward with its infrastructure. He knew growth would come where infrastructure was in place. For example, he coined the phrase "Lowe's to Lowe's Water Project". He envisioned a 10 inch water line on Route 19/460 since that is our main corridor and an area for growth. At the time we could have served most of the Route 19/460 Corridor with a smaller line size but he knew that one day the larger line would be needed.

Now many years later, the county is developing the Bluestone which is a 680 acre mixed use development. It has been called an urban development in a rural setting. This development will be served by the water line installed on Route 19/460.

By thinking ahead many years ago, the water line is sized for this development and no upgrades along the Route 19/460 Corridor will be needed.

This is just one example of his vision.

DON'S STORY – JOYCE McCONNELL

When I began working as secretary for Don Dunford in August of 1978, I certainly didn't expect to work there for thirty years, 6 months, and 2 weeks. It was with mixed emotions when I left in February 2009. It was a good to be able to retire, but I was leaving the employ of a man who is a dear friend, not only to me, but also to my family.

Joyce McConnell.

Working for Don was never dull or routine. The job required more than secretarial and bookkeeping skills. There were sinks and commodes to unclog, garbage disposals to restart, heat pumps and circuit breakers to reset, and other minor repairs to do for the tenants if Don was not around to do them

Don knows many people from all over. It was not unusual to get a call from someone in Texas, Washington, D.C., Florida, or other distant locations. These calls could be from people he had not heard from for maybe twenty or thirty years, and they just wanted to check in with an old friend. He leaves a memorable impression. My association with him has given me the opportunity to meet people from all walks of life.

It was tiring at times just to watch him when he was in the middle of a building project. He could have more energy than the Energizer Bunny. When he ran for political office, he would be the same the morning after the election whether he won or lost. If he lost, he just moved on to another project. If he won, he immediately set forth to do the best job he could for the people.

Don is a generous man, and I am fortunate to have been his employee. Most of all, I am fortunate to have his friendship.

DON'S STORY – LYNN CAMPBELL

When Lynn and her husband, Doug, were in search of a new place to live, Don Dunford came to her rescue.

During a cold and wintery Thanksgiving, the heat source in the home they were living in went out and the hopes of getting it repaired were hopeless.

Lynn and Doug had already begun a new home search and were planning to move into the newly constructed apartment building funded by Don Dunford.

A telephone call to Don from Lynn and Doug saved the day for them because he allowed them to move into their new apartment even though the construction had not been completed for the apartment building.

DON'S STORY – MARY LAWSON

Mary Lawson.

I spoke with Mary Lawson, Foundation Director of the Southwest Virginia Community College, about contributions made by Don and Nancy Dunford to the college.

"He was one of the first people in Southwest Virginia Community College service region to make a contribution to the college as a charitable institution, through an IRA.

"Don has also made a bequest through his Last Will and Testament upon his death to the college. With that Last Will and Testament contribution, he and his wife, Nancy, have become members of the Cornerstone Society.

"Nancy served on the College Board and her services were greatly appreciated

"Don and Nancy have endowed a scholarship for a Tazewell High School graduate to attend Southwest Virginia Community College.

"Of course, he was the reason Southwest Community College obtained a new building in the mid '70's, I believe. At that time only Buchanan Hall was in existence. Don called Dr. King asking him if he wanted a new building. That's how the funds for Tazewell Hall were obtained from the funds provided by the State of Virginia. It started with a telephone call from Don Dunford.

"Don and Nancy have been important assets to Southwest Virginia Community College."

DON'S STORY – TOM AND BONNIE CASH

I work with Bonnie Cash and I can tell you that is a real pleasure.

She took it upon herself to gather some information for me about the interaction between her husband, Tom, and Don Dunford.

"Tom and Don worked together on the Board of Supervisors for Tazewell County and Don did a great job with getting the county roads prioritized and paved. He worked with the Virginia Department of Transportation (VDOT) to get many of the county roads adopted by the state so that the money would come from the state coffers not the county. They both felt it was a major project that needed to be done," explains Bonnie.

"The Cavitt's Creek project was one that brought in the National Guard to help with all of the work that had to be done to develop the park at no cost to the county. Tom said Don's help was invaluable.

"Don helped entice Wood Tech, a Japanese company, to open up for business in Falls Mills. They manufactured plastic wood and exported it to Japan.

"The development of the Wardell Industrial Park was pushed forward and Ceramic Technology Company and Rag Pickers were added to the industries in the park with Don's help.

"Tom liked working with Don because of the energy he possessed and his inexhaustible need to serve his community.

"Working on the Board of Supervisors is a thankless job but it was made bearable by the visions of Don Dunford. Don always had the interests of Tazewell County in his heart. The fact that he was a visionary and self-made man helped pave the way for Don to offer his advice and support for the future of Tazewell County," was how Tom explained Don Dunford, a friend.

"I have also had the pleasure of working with Don," said Bonnie. "My contact occurred when he formed the Tazewell County Free Press. He decided the county needed another expressed opinion for the people of the county to see and understand when it came to the important issues that were facing the county.

"I found Don easy to work for as I performed my duties of selling advertisements and delivering papers.

"Don never did anything half way. He was totally committed to the Tazewell County Free Press while he was at the helm."

DON'S STORY – JERRY WOOD

Jerry Wood - Town Manager.

Jerry Wood, Town Manager of the Town of Tazewell, tells me that he has known Don and Nancy Dunford since 1971 when they became across the street neighbors.

He said Don discussed with him several issues that were important to Tazewell County during Don's years in the Virginia Legislature.

"Don was always receptive to any idea or suggestion one might have. He worked for his county and the area he represented to the best of his ability.

"He fought to get the exits of the Route 460 to the Town of Tazewell and especially pushed to obtain the Carline Bridge Exit into the town.

"When I was on the Board of Supervisors I appointed Don Dunford to the PSA Board. The need for clean water was discussed and Don was assigned by the Legislature to a project that studied the need for good, clean water in Southwest Virginia.

"He was responsible for instigating the Lowes to Lowes Water Project that ran from Bluefield, Virginia to Richlands, Virginia. He worked tirelessly on this water project until it became a reality."

"I know that Don Dunford will give anything he can to the Town of Tazewell if it will be of benefit to the youth. He has donated to the town eight acres of land that we are in the process of developing into a public park. We are currently raising money for a pavilion with a picnic area for the youngsters to congregate and play. The park is located across the street from the new YMCA.

"His donations of land and money have aided many people in the Town of Tazewell as well as the County of Tazewell and all of us who are Virginians."

DON'S STORY – JIM THOMPSON

Jim Thompson.

Drinking buddies – coffee, that is. Much like our great friend and colleague the late Judge Fred Combs, Don is very much a creature of habit. It was once said that Judge Combs went through the same routine each day, "leaving his mark" along the way. Such is Don.

I first came to know Don in the late 1980's when my office became one of his regular daily stopping points. As we all know, Don was then, and remains, a very early riser, does his exercising, his breakfast, is at work by 7:00 AM, lines out his day's work, goes to the post office, and then, for many years, stopped by my office on Main Street for a cup of coffee. Knowing exactly where the pot was, he would stroll down the hallway wearing his VA Tech attire and with a cheerful whistle, pour himself a cup. He would then sit down with me and we would talk about the ways of the world and attempt to solve all its problems.

It was then that I came to realize what an accomplished and successful businessman Don is, and what an astute politician he remains.

Don has certainly utilized his God-given talents in a marvelous way to make Tazewell County and this region a better place to live. Whether it has been through the State Legislature or the Tazewell County Board of Supervisors, the Tazewell County, PSA, and other community/civic projects, Don has, and continues to 'LEAVE HIS MARK" on our region in a very positive way.

DON'S STORY - WOODROW MULLINS

As Superintendent of Schools for 10 years and in Public Administration for 35 years in Tazewell County Public Schools, I had the pleasure of knowing Don Dunford. Don was instrumental in school renovations during my years in the school system. He organized a bus tour and had the Board of Supervisors, Legislative Officials and community leaders taken to each of the county schools to do a walk through to point out the needs of repair. He was a great friend to public education in Tazewell County and was able to convince the Board of Supervisors to allocate funding for remodeling each of the schools.

Don has the gift of having good ol' country boy sense as well as good economic sense. His business ways are very aggressive and straight forward. Don knows what he wants and goes all out to get it. He is very community oriented and very verbal about the direction of things going wrong in his community.

Woodrow & Betty Mullins.

On the flip side, Don has one of the biggest hearts of anyone I know. I remember watching him take care of his Dad when was ill. He took his Dad breakfast every morning and made sure he was comfortable and had everything he needed. That told me a lot about the kind of person Don Dunford really was.

Don is a big fan and supporter of Virginia Tech. I remember a time when he held a cookout at his home for all of the coaches at Tech. That was impressive.

Don has been a great friend of mine over the years and a big influence in my politics as well as in my life. I am proud to say that Don Dunford is my friend.

Coyote Kill - Happy Farmers.

Phil & Peggy Averett.

Averetts & Dunfords at Mountain Lake.

Jack & Bonnie Sisk.

Jim & Joan Doak.

Wade & Virginia Coates.

Eddie & Mary Ellen McGraw.

Judge & Mrs. Fred Combs.

Joyce & Al Gillespie.

Bill & Peggy Foster.

Jack & Helen Hawks.

John Rupe & Diane Santolla.

The Mountains of Tazewell County

*Joyce McConnel - Don's Secretary of 31 years with
Marci & Bill.*

Friends & Neighbors H.S. & Pam Caudill.

Don Dunford, Billy Hite, Doug Hess.

Coach Billy Hite, Coach Lorenzo Ward, Don Dunford.

Dick Bowman, Jack Sisk, Al Gillespie, Don Dunford, Wade Coates at Race Trip at Claiborne Farms in Kentucky.

Fred Combs, Fred Dean, Russell Hatfield, Elena Combs.

Sisks, Fosters, Gillespies, & Averetts.

A Beautiful Tailgate.

Fred & Iva Dean.

Phil & Diane Averett.

John & Patty Glavaris.

Don & Jean Walk.

Claude & Betty Van Dyke.

BILL PEERY'S MOTTO:

Life should NOT be a journey to the grave with the intention of
Arriving safely in an attractive and well preserved body, but rather
To skid in sideways, a woman in one hand, Early Times in the other, body
Thoroughly used up, totally worn out and screaming
"WOO HOO, what a ride!"

THE LEGISLATOR'S PRAYER

Oh Lord that I might be granted the wisdom of Al Philpott,

the wit the Tom Moss,

the oratorical ability of Ray Garland,

the tenacity of Mary Marshall,

the sincerity of Bunny Gunn,

the blaze'ness of Lewis McMurran,

the gentility of Orby Cantrell,

the charisma of Lacey Putney,

the self control of the Speaker,

the earthiness of Don Dunford,

the money of Norman Sisisky,

and the luck of Jim Thompson,

and if we're fortunate enough not to have opposition maybe I could be

reelected.

                                        AUTHOR UNKNOWN

CHAPTER 17

A Word of Thanks

At the end of the first chapter of this book, I wrote "I AM IM-PRESSED." Well, I think that needs to be said again. While pursuing the happenings in the life of Don Dunford, I have had the pleasure of talking to many fine, wonderful people who were so very willing to say a few words on Don's behalf.

Many of those people offered words that I included in Chapter 17, and many more were verbal wishes of good will.

I now am very proud to be able to call Don Dunford my friend and I pray that he sees me in he same light.

Thank you to all of you.

Linda Hudson Hoagland - Author

September 1, 1991

Bluefield, Va.

Mr. Don Dunford, Member Board of Supervisors

Tazewell County Virginia

Dear Don:

I want to label you the 20 Million Dollar Man. This is the amount that you saved Tazewell County last month in your forceful showing that Graham High School is in better shape than Cosby, Reasor, and Dudley had led the people of Bluefield to believe.

I am attaching my drawing of the small wart on the floor of Graham High School rather than the huge sink-hole that Cosby had people believing would swallow the entire school at a moments notice. The room could be repaired, locked shut and forgotten for another 30 years.

The first depression in the floor occured about 8 years ago and the hole was enlarged with jack hammers to about 6 x 6 and filled with concrete and forgotten. Three years ago an addition of 1 Million dollars in Library and Science rooms were added (no problem). Last year an elevator at a cost of 50 thousand dollars was added (no problem). Last year the heating system was converted from Coal to Natural Gas (No problem).

Here are some to the reports made at School Board Meetings:

Nov. 13, 1989   Marshall Miller said the school should have never been built in the present location (After 30 years). He said $34,000 Roof Drainage repairs and $26,000. to repair the small wart in the floor. He stated the building is SAFE. In 1991 he says to move over 20 feet and build a new school.

Feb. 6, 1990   Corte Construction Co. given contract to repair the wart. Mr. Corte told me (No big deal). Work to be done after June closing of school for summer. Cost (not published ?).

June, 1990   Contract halted.

July 9, 1990   Cosby stated that it is Impossible to completely repair Graham High School.

July 18, 1990   Cosby stated that it would cost 3 Million dollars just to reinforce the footers. Footers that were suitable for 30 years.

Aug. 14, 1991   Estimate now close to $100,000, very much lower than untold millions.

I have seen sink holes within 1/4 Mile of Graham High School filled with dirt and rock. I have seen similiar holes in Abbs Valley and Russell County filled and forgotten.

In conclussion I have never witnessed such a down to earth presentation that you made to the School Board in August 1991. What you did in one half hours completely educated people that had been brain washed for over two years with untruths and statements that could not be proven.

Sincerely,

Russell Garrett

108 Allendale St.

JAMES P. EDWARDS
QUAIL VILLAGE
10339 QUAIL CROWN DRIVE
NAPLES, FLORIDA 34119
PHONE (941) 597-6231

October 22, 2004

The Honorable Donald Dunford
P. O. Box 60
Tazewell, Va., 24651

Dear Don:

I wish to express my deepest gratitude for your representation of the fighting ninth and especially your assistance in getting our Airport; but more importantly; the role you played, in. retaining the Department of Aviation while serving as a member of the House of Delegates.

I think it is important that other members of the Aviation Commission be advised of how you stood up for Aviation in Virginia and due to the importance of Aviation; you would not use or make a political issue of your action. Let's review your important role.

Tazewell County Board of Supervisors authorized an Airport Commission and I was selected as Chairman. This was the time that Governor Dalton had been elected Governor. I received a call from Colonel Plentl, Director of Aviation, who advised that the Governor desired to change transportation in our state by forming a new Department of Transportation. The Aviation Commission under the Judicial Department would be relocated under the Highway Department. This would have been a terrible move for Aviation. Colonel Plentl wanted help for Aviation.

To make a long story short, I called you, explained the problem and I will never forget your words. Jim, the bill is in my hopper and it will stay there until you tell me Aviation will be satisfactory to you and the Aviation Commission. **THIS YOU DID!**

A short time later, I had a Call from Governor Dalton wanting to know what he could do to get his bill through. We had a long conversation, whereby, I explained what we had was working great for aviation. The Judges loved working with the Commission and placing Aviation Under the Highway Department was a No. No. as it was difficult to get a sign put up much less getting an airport built under their regulations. He was very nice and said he would look into the problem and get back with me. A few days later he called back and we had a nice chat. I told the Governor, the Department of Aviation had to be equal and separate to the Highway Department without any connection, except a part of the Department of Transportation. He seemed at that time to be satisfied. I believe we made a friend. He later appointed me to the Commission and called often for news on the proposed airport and Southwest Virginia

I thank you and hope your health and strength will be spared through many years which you may continue to exercise assistance to those seeking success in the business world. You are a GREAT ANERICAN,

With Kindest Personal Regards,

CY; Commission Members

Advanced Technology:
Carilion Roanoke Memorial Hospital Leading the Way in Cardiac Care

A Heartfelt Partnership

Don Dunford (above), of Tazewell, woke up last October at 2:30 a.m. after he felt like he had been "kicked by a mule in the chest."

It was the first sign of an impending heart attack. He woke his wife, Nancy. His intention was to get to his cardiologist in Roanoke, John C. Lystash, M.D., when the office opened. But he only made it as far as Bluefield Regional Medical Center (BRMC), choosing to go to the emergency room there instead of chancing the long drive.

While undergoing tests at the medical center, he had a heart attack "on the table" but never lost consciousness. After medication and further testing, it was determined he needed a five-way bypass.

Dunford told the ER physician he wanted to go to Carilion Roanoke Memorial Hospital (CRMH) so Dr. Lystash could take care of him.

Luckily for Dunford, he was at the hospital when he had the heart attack. Thankfully, too, BRMC and CRMH are members of HeartNet of the Virginias. For 15 years, hospitals and physicians from southwest Virginia and eastern West Virginia have teamed together as HeartNet of the Virginias to improve treatment for their cardiac patients.

"From the minute the ambulance picked me up in Bluefield to my admittance at CRMH, it was a smooth process. Both hospitals worked well together to get me the care I needed," Dunford said.

Following the five-way bypass procedure by cardiovascular surgeon D. Christopher Wells, M.D., and follow-up care with Dr. Lystash, Dunford says today he feels better than he has in years.

"I feel like I am 35 years old again," he said.

Robotic Surgery: High-Tech for the Heart

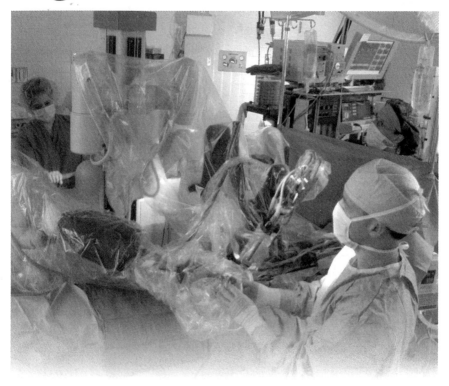

Carilion Roanoke Memorial Hospital is one of a few hospitals nationwide to treat heart patients with the da Vinci Surgical System. This advanced system functions with three robotic arms and a high-resolution stereoscopic viewing system. Patients receiving bypass surgery or other heart procedures benefit with faster recovery times, less post-operative pain and fewer complications. For more information about our robotic heart surgery, visit www.carilion.com and click on our Heart Care link.

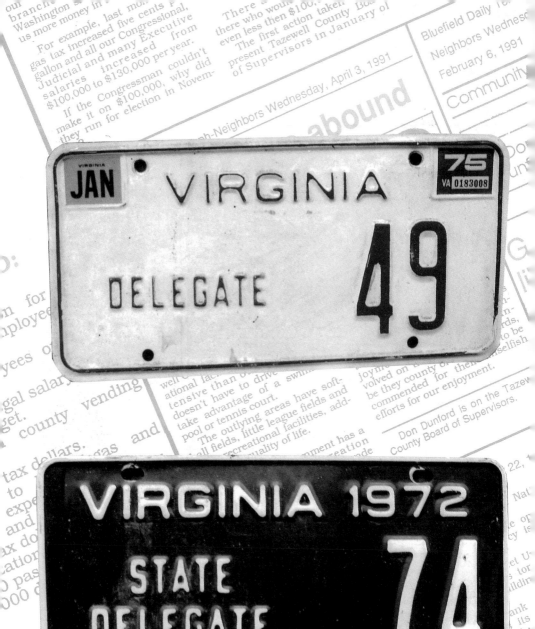

Nancy & Donna.

VT Football 2010

Don Pictured with Charlie Wiles & Brian Steinspring, 3-24-2010.

Don & Travis Wells, WDBJ-TV (Channel 7) Sports Director, one of Don's old tailgate buddies.

Don & Tyrod ready for Spring game 2010.

Bobby Goss.

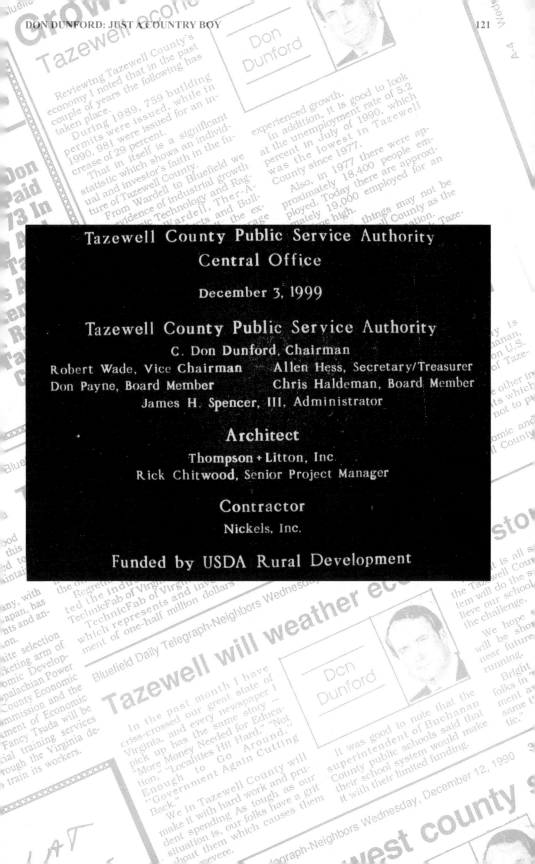

Tazewell County Public Service Authority
Central Office

December 3, 1999

Tazewell County Public Service Authority

C. Don Dunford, Chairman

Robert Wade, Vice Chairman — Allen Hess, Secretary/Treasurer

Don Payne, Board Member — Chris Haldeman, Board Member

James H. Spencer, III, Administrator

Architect

Thompson + Litton, Inc.

Rick Chitwood, Senior Project Manager

Contractor

Nickels, Inc.

Funded by USDA Rural Development

Virginia State Capitol.